To
My mother
Lois Ann Fincher
Whose life taught me to live with questions

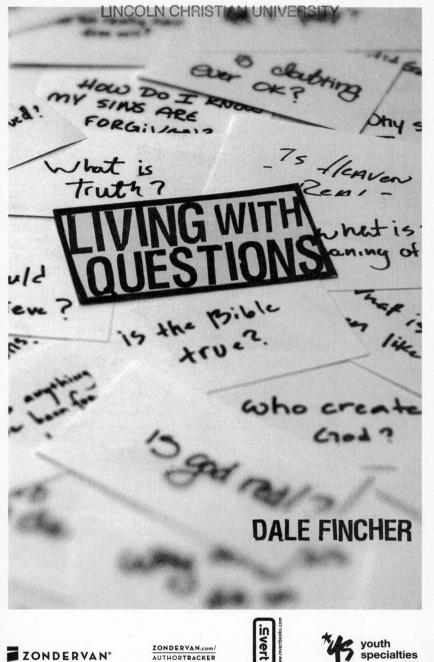

LIVING WITH QUESTIONS

DALE FINCHER

Living with Questions
Copyright © 2007 by Charles Dale Fincher

Youth Specialties products, 300 S. Pierce St., El Cajon, CA 92020 are published by Zondervan, 5300 Patterson Ave. SE, Grand Rapids, MI 49530.

Library of Congress Cataloging-in-Publication Data
Fincher, Dale.
  Living with questions / by Dale Fincher.
    p. cm.
  ISBN-10: 0-310-27664-0 (pbk.)
  ISBN-13: 978-0-310-27664-7 (pbk.)
1. Christian teenagers—Religious life. I. Title.
  BV4531.3.F547 2007
  248.8'3—dc22

                                                              2007017042

Published in association with the literary agency of Alive Communications, Inc., 7680 Goddard Street, Suite 200, Colorado Springs, Colorado 80920, www.alivecommunications.com.

All Scripture quotations, unless otherwise indicated, are taken from the *Holy Bible: New International Version*®. NIV®. Copyright © 1973, 1978, 1984 by International Bible Society. Used by permission of Zondervan. All rights reserved.

Web site addresses listed in this book were current at the time of publication. Please contact Youth Specialties via e-mail (YS@YouthSpecialties.com) to report URLs that are no longer operational and provide replacement URLs if available.

Creative Team: Dave Urbanski, Laura Gross, David Conn, Brad Taylor, and Anna Hammond
Cover Design by SharpSeven Design

Printed in the United States of America

08 09 10 11 12 • 23 22 21 20 19 18 17 16 15 14 13 12 11 10 9 8 7 6 5 4

> Live the questions now. Perhaps then, someday far in the future, you will gradually, without even noticing it, live your way into the answer.
> —Rainer Maria Rilke, *Letters to a Young Poet*

CONTENTS

PREFACE

A TALE OF TWO FRIENDS

CJ lived next door to Max since the fifth grade. In those early days, the whole world seemed to lie right outside their front doors. They'd ride their bikes to the grocery store to buy baseball cards. On weekends they'd sleep at each other's houses and build forts by draping sheets across their bedrooms. They played video games when homerun derby in the street got rained out. As they grew into their teenage years, the games didn't change—they only got more complicated.

When the pair pulled CJ's silver Cadillac into a parking lot by the beach, a parking attendant from the nearby restaurant shouted, "Get daddy's car off my lot!"

Max waved his arms out the passenger window and shouted back, "This isn't his dad's car! It's *his*!" CJ screeched the tires as they bumped over the curb and headed back into traffic. Driving the Caddy embarrassed CJ, even though he was the first one of his friends to have wheels. So to make up for not having a sports car, he'd rev the engine in neutral and then kick it into drive to make the tires squeal.

CJ received his mom's hand-me-down vehicle when he was 16—the day after the dentist removed his braces, in fact. The car even came with cloth seats and imitation wood trim—the complete package. CJ used his Christmas and birthday money to rig the car with subwoofers in the trunk. It thumped down the street so loudly that Max nicknamed it "The Trunk of Funk."

On the weekends, CJ and Max spent a lot of time with Stephen and their other friends just leaning against the hood of that Cadillac in the parking lot of Taco Bell.

"What are you guys doing?" kids would ask as they pulled up.

"Nothin'."

The usual reply. If they'd been doing something, then they wouldn't be standing in a parking lot. But it was a good place to plan, hang with the people, and meet girls.

* * * *

CJ grew up with his mom and younger sister. His father moved out when CJ was six. His sister pestered him endlessly at home, always annoying him from his bedroom doorway until he was angry enough to knuckle her on the arm. Then she'd tell their mom, and that usually earned CJ a reprimand.

Worse than home, though, were CJ's weekend visits with his dad every couple of months. When he went to his father's place in the country, he felt stuffed inside an alien world. CJ just wanted to hang with his friends back in his neighborhood, not feel trapped with grown-ups.

CJ liked Max because he was one of the few friends who didn't insult CJ when other guys were around. Max also didn't compete with CJ or try to prove he was better than him—unlike many of CJ's other friends. They didn't even compete with each other in sports—CJ was the basketball player, and Max was the football player.

They saw the world in the same way, too, which made CJ trust Max even more. And when it came to laughing, they generated enough inside jokes and sayings to make a recording on an old cassette tape. They were equals—blood brothers for life.

Though CJ attended a Christian school, he spent little time with his classmates off campus. His neighborhood friends were far more interesting. They grew up together through elementary, middle, and now high school. His friends attended public school, and they came home with stories that sounded like headlines from a newspaper.

"Did you hear about Stephen? He got so drunk on Friday that he was puking in the back seat of Ashley's car!" They'd all laugh about it together.

CJ wondered what it would be like to get drunk, and he wondered if Ashley was laughing, too.

* * * *

One day, before the Trunk of Funk era, Max took CJ to his dad's bedroom closet. Inside were piles of pornographic magazines—stacked in rows that towered above their heads. There were more magazines than clothes.

Something deep in CJ's gut rebelled.

This isn't right! he thought to himself. *But Max's dad thinks it's fine. And Max's dad is a war veteran, a strong guy, and he still lives in Max's house. Do these pictures bother Max? Why are we sneaking around? What if we get caught? Is that the front door opening and closing? Max had better hurry up anyway.*

Max navigated the closet as though he'd done it before. He pulled down a magazine and thumbed through the pages. At that moment, CJ knew he was the only sheltered person standing in the closet.

Max is all right, CJ thought. *He sticks with me...but my stomach aches. I shouldn't look at this stuff. But I'm curious. Just a little curious. It won't hurt me to just look.*

They took a few of the magazines and put them in Max's closet. Two months later, CJ turned 15.

Through those years, CJ and Max savored the more complicated pleasures of their self-made world. They listened to rap music from a ghetto-oppressed African-American culture they pictured in their heads. They enjoyed military-themed movies and hitting mailboxes with baseball bats. They loved the idea of civil rebellion and hatred of the police, although they never attended a protest and rarely encountered the authorities.

At home, CJ grew persistently more rude and argumentative toward his mother and sister. His mind moved with belligerence and anger. His best weapon was his sharp and deprecating tongue. His mother disapproved of his music, mysterious capers, and friends; but she rarely made demands besides going to church on Sunday, eating dinner together each weeknight, and a midnight curfew on the weekends.

* * * *

When Halloween came, CJ's mother asked him to take his sister to a Halloween-alternative party at their church.

"Mom! Come on, that's boring! I don't *want* to do that!" he exclaimed. His mother consented under his onslaught of words.

CJ, now alone in the house, met Max at the front door before sunset.

"Do you have the bottles?" Max asked. CJ grinned. He'd filled them that afternoon with the acid used to balance the chemicals in the swimming pool. Stuffing the bottles into the cargo pockets of their camouflage fatigues, CJ and Max strolled onto the dusky streets.

A white van tore around the corner and stopped in the middle of the street beside a black sports car. From the car window came obscene gestures, and then the guys in the van threw raw eggs at the car.

Max knew the guys in the van, including the driver, Jason. Max introduced them to CJ, and then he and CJ climbed aboard.

The van circled the block and stopped in a new neighborhood. The guys slammed open the van doors and rushed a group of trick-or-treating children, including an unsuspecting Cinderella and her brother the Pumpkin. Max fisted two eggs. CJ grabbed one. Not wanting to hurt the youngsters, CJ lagged behind just enough to be harmless, yet appear malicious. A sprint through a field, some squeals, and a few dropped bags of candy were enough to please these guys. They returned to the waiting van and cruised into another subdivision.

Max shared the secret about what he and CJ were carrying in their cargo pockets.

"What an idea!" Jason exclaimed. CJ played along.

So the six of them crawled out of the parked van. Darting under shadows, they clustered under a hedgerow across the street from their target.

"Do you know this house?" asked CJ.

"No," said the boys.

Max pulled out his acid bottle. They mixed the chemicals to create a reaction; then one guy bolted across the street, opened the mailbox, and shoved the bottle inside before hurrying back. The boys huddled together under a bush and held their breath.

The bomb's explosion pierced the night, and it was soon followed by the sound of car alarm sirens and the glare of porch lights as the neighbors investigated the noise.

The grass hardly bent under CJ's speedy feet, and nobody dared to glance back. They regrouped at the van. No adults sighted.

As the evening waned, the neighborhood children went indoors. It was a school night. Time to go home. The streets settled.

They would first drop off CJ and Max. They drove through Hollyfield and turned down Fawn Lane. Then they took a left onto Mulberry. A flashing blue light suddenly tailed them. They all cursed. CJ took his extra bottle of acid and threw it deep under the seats. His mind raced for alternative stories to the mailbox explosion.

If I play it politely and respectfully, he thought, *maybe I can dodge the trouble.*

The van pulled to the curb, and the boys piled out. Two police cars stopped behind the van with their flashing lights reflecting off the nearby windows where neighbors watched.

"This white van has been reported for vandalizing with eggs," said the officer.

"Some people threw eggs at us, too!" Jason exclaimed as he took a step toward the cop.

Without flinching, the officer continued, "I want you to dump all the eggs into the street."

Claiming no ownership to the eggs, CJ backed against the curb and stayed behind the boys as they emptied the cartons onto the pavement. He hoped the officer wouldn't find that bottle of acid under the van seats and trace it back to the mailbox.

"Is that all of the eggs?" the officer boomed.

They nodded.

"Are you sure? If I find any more eggs in this vehicle, you're in serious trouble. Are you certain these are all the eggs?"

They nodded again. The mess of white and yellow streamed into the gutter.

The officer reached into the car, wrestled through some empty cartons, and pulled out a dozen fresh eggs. The boys groaned.

"You can't do this!" Jason protested. He moved between the officer and the van. Without hesitation, the officer pushed and then pinned Jason against the hood.

"I'm sick of punks like you!" he said. "You are under arrest. In fact, because of him, you're *all* under arrest."

CJ froze.

For the first time that he could remember, he felt like he was on the wrong side.

The officers searched the van with eager flashlights. They found other illegal goods, including weapons and a blue-flashing light that impersonated the ones still spinning on the police cars.

You know that hopeless feeling you get when there's no way out? How you wish you could just disappear? You wish you could undo the past couple of hours and delete the trouble you're in now. You wish you'd had no adventure and that you were safe at a church party or even under the covers in your own bed. That's how CJ felt.

He looked at the street sign on the corner—Mulberry Way and Grover Lane. He was only two blocks from home. *What does this mean?* he thought. *Are we being handcuffed? Am I going to jail? How do I get out of this? How do I hide this from Mom? Why couldn't the cops have pulled the van over two minutes later, when I'd be home and away from the trouble? Why is Max's friend being an idiot and yelling at the cops? Why didn't they dump all the eggs?*

Then CJ sensed the world slowing down. The police escorted the boys toward the patrol cars one by one. One was handcuffed and pinned against the van. Another recited his address to the policeman. CJ felt alone. Max had failed him. Their favorite rap music with its "f--- tha police" lyrics now sounded small and tinny in CJ's mind.

Then the prayer that was waiting in CJ's chest came through.

God, help me!

A voice from within returned just as quickly: *Why should I help you? So you can make my name* small *in the earth?*

All escapes were now closed.

In those few moments spent watching the officer scribble down his name and watching his friends get shoved into the squad cars, CJ's emotions intensified and he realized something shockingly clear. If there was a purpose to life, this wasn't it. This was not new and improved, sophisticated, helpful, safe, or sane. It was nasty, brutish, and lonely.

* * * *

When CJ finally returned home, his mother scolded him. She blamed herself for not insisting that he go to the party at church. She walked up the street to Max's house and briefly spoke with Max's dad. Then she came home again, discouraged by his hands-off attitude. All the while, she was unaware of the things now happening in CJ's soul and the new questions that lived there.

A daunting question kept ringing in his mind: *How should I live?* While he wrestled with that thought shut inside his room, he discovered other questions that needed to be answered first: *Do ideas really matter? Isn't it enough that my friends like me and let me hang with them in the parking lot on weekends? If ideas matter so much, then which ones are the true ideas and how would I know? Does my life need to line up with the truth? How? Does God exist? If so, does God listen? Does God care?* These questions all needed answers before CJ could make sense of his first question.

CJ then became afraid, more afraid than he'd ever been before—even while he was being arrested on the street.

I feel thrown into existence, CJ thought, *and I don't know why.* To the center of his soul, it haunted him.

He needed some time before he could formulate any answers. So he knocked them around in his head. He began to read for himself. He learned to listen to different voices, not just the voices of his friends or the rap artists.

CJ hung out with Max later that week, but it all felt different. More weeks passed. CJ holed up in his room a lot, where he mostly journaled and explored other kinds of music.

Max knocked on the front door after school one day.

"Hey, what's up?" CJ asked.

"We're goin' over to Stephen's. Wanna come?"

"No, you guys go ahead."

"What's wrong with you, man?" Max voiced the same question rumbling in CJ's soul.

CJ didn't have an answer. "Nothin', really," he shrugged. "I just don't feel like goin'." That was all he could say.

"All riiiight. Seeee ya."

CJ closed the door…and ended an era. He watched through the window as Max stepped off the porch and walked across the driveway. He met up with some other guys, and they all moved slowly up the street.

CJ and Max's friendship never recovered.

* * * *

CJ's story isn't unique. Many people have needed their worlds shattered to help them wake up to the real stuff of life.

But you don't have to experience a shattered world to start taking life seriously. You have the choice to ask your own questions—right now.

Look at your life. *What is your story? Where are you? What matters most to you?*

Listen to yourself. *What would devastate you if it were removed? Your driving privileges? Your friends? Your own bedroom? Your clothing style? Your cell phone? Your music? Your freedom? Why would it hurt you?*

Be honest about your fears, pain, and desires for living the way you do.

Socrates, the famous Greek philosopher, told us, "The unexamined life is not worth living." Just like CJ, the police eventually arrested Socrates, too. They even poisoned him. But unlike CJ, Socrates lived an examined life. And unlike CJ, he'd discovered some of the stuff of real life that was worth living and dying for.

Examine your life and see what comes to mind.

Here are some questions to help you begin:

What would the ideal life look like for you?

What's good about your life?

What do you want more than anything else in life?

What does it mean to be happy?

If you could change one habit in your life, what would it be?

What's the one thing you cannot live without?

What has hurt you most in life?

When you're sad or lonely, what do you turn to? Friends? Music? Reading? Alcohol? Cutting?

CJ started living with questions when all the escapes were cut off. But rather than being confined, he found a new thirst for life. In fact, CJ found that the answers to his questions grew broader, deeper, more colorful, and more meaningful as time passed. They started filling the empty spaces of his soul.

How do I know?

I am CJ.

INTRODUCTION

LET'S MAKE A DEAL

The hard thing about something as personal and important as the topic of this book is how to talk about it.

Living with questions is humbling. It makes us vulnerable because we're admitting that we're uncertain—even afraid.

Writing about this topic is also hard. On the one hand, I'm tempted to just be fun and win you over. I want you to like me.

On the other hand, I'm tempted to be firm and sober. This is serious stuff.

To me, both sides are a bit off. So let's aim down the middle. I promise to be myself—and shoot straight with these serious questions. But that will only work if you interact with these pages with honesty and the expectation that a wide frontier is just around the corner.

Deal?

If that's no deal, then please feel free to put this book back on the shelf. If you're not asking the hard questions, if you're not feeling perplexed by trying to find your purpose in life, if you're not struggling to find at least one person who can relate to your need to find answers, then this book is probably not for you. Go watch a movie, and return whenever you're ready.

WHERE DO I BEGIN?

Are you still with me? Okay, then—what are you looking for? Are you living with questions? Are you on a quest to understand something bigger about life? What do you hope to find?

The word *question* comes from the word *quest*. And finding out what's right about the world is a quest. It's like searching for a treasure with a map, gradually filling in the answers with each step closer to the big **X**.

When I was a teenager, there were times when I felt frustrated, lonely, and scared. I also lacked the confidence to ask many people for the answers to my questions because I was afraid I'd sound stupid. I figured that if I were going to suffer alone, then it was better to do it without people thinking I was weird.

So I searched for a book that would help me find some answers to my questions because I couldn't voice them very well yet. I visited a small bookshop to look for something that might help me. Staring at the tall tower of books that stretched up from my toes to the ceiling, I thought to myself, *Where do I begin?* Maybe you have the same question. Or maybe you've already been asking a few people—your friends, teachers, mentors, or parents.

Were their answers too simple? Did they dodge your questions because they weren't confident of their answers? Did they suggest that you "take it all by faith" or not "make everything so serious"? Or did they say, "God's thoughts are above your thoughts, so don't even try to understand them"?

Madeleine L'Engle, a writer I came to respect, said she spent most of her life undoing bad ideas that were taught to her by well-intentioned adults.[1]

I've been discouraged by this thought ever since I became serious about life. Many people, including adults, don't take the time to ask difficult questions or, even worse, to find the answers. Or they're too easily satisfied with simple answers.

And many ignore their questions altogether, finding it easier to plug into electronic distractions. This is disheartening to many of us who are sincere about our questions.

In fact, many have found no answers in their friends, teachers, or parents and have therefore concluded that answers must not exist.

In my travels, I've asked student audiences to write down their two most important questions in life—questions that, if they were answered, would make life a little easier. I've collected several thousand questions. Some of the most popular and most important of them are the backbone of this book.

You are not alone. You are not alone in your questions. You are not alone as you learn to live into the answers.

---

[1] Madeleine L'Engle, *Walking on Water: Reflections on Faith and Art.*

We were created with physical hunger, so we search for food to satisfy that hunger, find it, and eat it. In the same way, we were created with an intellectual hunger that comes in the form of deep questions. So we search for the answers to satisfy that hunger—and the answers must exist somewhere. There is food for the body and food for the mind. We must either find it or waste away.[2]

DOUBT

Some people struggle with doubt. They question things in life, feel guilty about asking, and then suppress any further questions because they're told "doubting is wrong."

Let me just say it now: Doubt is not immoral, nor is it wrong.[3] It's struggling to find out what is true. Living with questions is partly about doubt. It's also partly about taking steps on the quest toward finding that treasure of truth.

Doubt is a fire alarm that says something doesn't make sense.

Doubt pushes us into our quest—even when ignoring our doubts sounds more comfortable at the moment.

Doubt is what gives us the motivation to face our fears and see if we have the courage to venture into dark places.

Doubt is often a friend who says "everything is *not* okay, so let's find a place that is."

Besides, everyone lives with doubt to some degree, even under very ordinary circumstances in their daily lives. People wonder, *Did my husband say he was going to pick up the kids from school? Did I recharge my iPod? Did I write down the correct answer on today's quiz? Did he really mean he* liked *that movie?*

Doubt happens, and we all do it. So let's not fret over it. After all, there's something far more tragic than doubting—refusing to deal with the truth when you know it's staring you in the face. We've all heard of immoral behavior. Well, refusing to deal with truth is immoral *intellectual* behavior. Doubt is a bundle of questions about the map and the journey; stubbornness dishonestly tears up the treasure map altogether.

---

[2] A form of this idea comes from C.S. Lewis, *Mere Christianity*.
[3] Jude 22, "Be merciful to those who doubt."

My journey with questions has been a lonely road at times. Sometimes it's been a difficult one, like the times when I've been in a dark tunnel of doubt feeling like a treasure hunter standing in a pitch-black cave and wondering if the treasure really exists. But I've gone through those times and come out of those caves with some nuggets in my pocket.

WAYS TO USE THIS BOOK

This book was written to help you start your journey of living with questions. Or, if you've already begun the journey, to help fill in some gaps and encourage you to keep going.

Each chapter got its inspiration from a question asked by a student. What I write are suggestions to consider and new perspectives to think about as you discover the answers that satisfy you.

Some chapters overlap others, as the concepts are all interwoven. It's interesting how concepts such as *faith, grace, love, sin, justice, brokenness, hope, glory*, and other such words, are interconnected.

I recommend reading the chapters in order. The first chapters are foundational and will help you dig deeper into later chapters. But if you do need to jump ahead, that's okay, too.

If you're looking for practical help, I've listed some suggestions and additional questions at the end of each chapter so you can do them on your own.

And if you're the studious type, at the back of the book I've also listed some resources for you to investigate. The more time you put into studying and exploring your own questions, the more confident and secure you'll be as you discover the answers.

Also look for the section of lined pages at the end of each chapter. As you're reading, write down the thoughts and questions that come to your mind. Those pages are for you to fill up. Perhaps some day you'll find some answers that you can scribble next to your questions.

One more thing: I'm a philosopher and a Christian. Therefore, what I write in these pages is from my perspective as a Christian. However,

I'm not a Christian because I was born that way nor because my family believed it. I'm a Christian because the more I tested the Christian way, the more satisfied I became that Christianity is closer to explaining real life than anything else.

Yet, even though I write as a Christian, this book isn't intended for only Christian readers; it's for anyone living with questions.

As you read you'll find that for several of the questions I give consideration to non-Christian points of view. While some other perspectives are certainly appealing, I've found that they aren't offering anything better than what I've found in Jesus Christ.

So explore with me. And even if you're skeptical of Christian ideas, at least in these pages you'll receive an honest perspective from a questioner whose journey led him to the person of Jesus.

KEEPING YOUR BEST QUESTIONS ALIVE

In life, some questions are more important than others. When a mountain climber is scaling the cliff's edge, "Where is my next hold?" is a more important question than, "Did I pack an extra energy bar?" The first question needs immediate attention. The second question can be asked on the mountaintop when there's time to rummage through the backpack.

In a way, we're all climbing a mountain.

And like a climber, we need the tools that will help us in the fiercest situations. Rocks may crumble and break off above the climber's head. And in our daily lives, we have many pressures that will knock us down if we're not alert. Friends will often silence our deep-down questions, or we may no longer feel accepted if we start asking questions that nobody around us cares about.

The climber needs to keep his gear accessible and maintained at all times, and we also need to keep our heads about us so we aren't gullible enough to believe everything we read on the Internet, hear from our friends, or enjoy in our music—no matter how much it tickles our ears.

We think about life because we want a good one. Like the climber, we want a summit worth climbing. Yet what a waste it would be for us to coast through life without giving any thought to purpose, meaning, pleasure, pain, and happiness. "Eat, drink, and be merry, for tomorrow we die!"[4]

Maybe you've experienced this sort of life—fat with pleasure and drunk with the spontaneity of living only for the moment, only to look back and realize the pleasure was thin and the passion without heart.

We must turn to the serious, personal question: *What is your purpose in life? Is your answer big enough to die for?* Or even better, *Is your answer big enough to* **live** *for? Is it big enough to live throughout the rest of your life and beyond?*

I hope that as you read this book you'll open your mind a little wider, you'll see the world from different perspectives, and you'll find hearty help to your questions. One famous writer said the reason we're open minded is the same reason we're open mouthed: To bite down on something solid.[5] Now let's chew on some big ideas.

QUESTIONS FOR YOU

What are your two most pressing questions in life? The kind that, if they were answered, would make life a little easier?

Is doubt wrong? Why or why not?

---

[4] The Dave Matthews Band sings this phrase (that's actually found in the Bible—Luke 12:19) as a poor way to live.
[5] G.K. Chesterton, *Autobiography*.

How is doubt like a fire alarm?

Have you ever faced your doubts? How did that change you?

What keeps you from asking the important questions?

What chapter in this book looks the most interesting to you?

QUESTION 1

DOES WHAT I THINK REALLY MATTER?

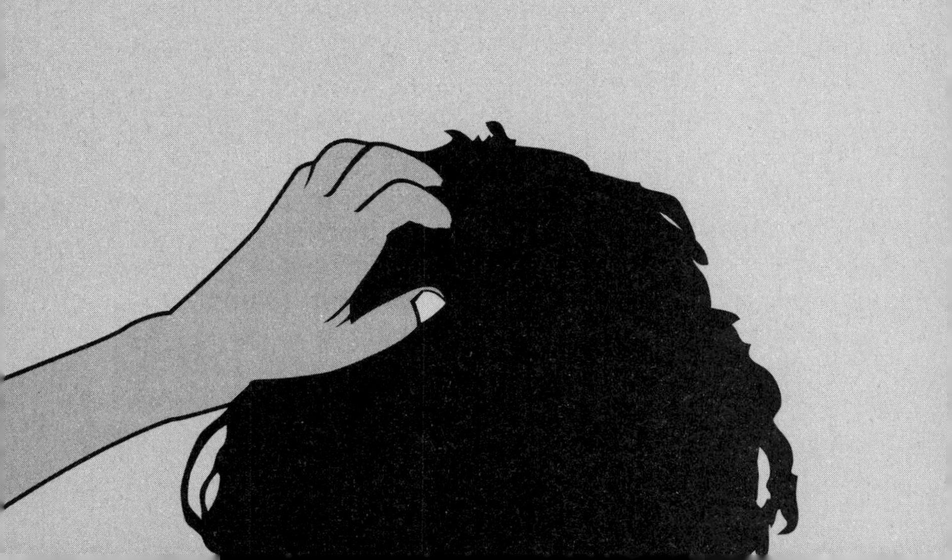

THE WORLDS WE MAKE

PROTECTING YOUR VILLAGE FROM THE DRAGON IS WAY MORE IMPORTANT THAN YOUR JOB.

That sentence was printed on a Mountain Dew banner that hung outside the Electronic Entertainment Expo, also known as "E3," in Los Angeles.

I laughed. *What does THAT have to do with Mountain Dew?* I thought. *And who really needs an excuse to play another video game?*

The kinds of gamers who attend E3 log dozens of hours every week to build up their massive, multiplayer online characters. Others enjoy the shorter rounds in first-person shooters (my personal favorite). And if they aren't shooting Nazis or practicing wizardry, then they're coordinating a simulated family (*The Sims*) or moving their dancing feet in sync with directional arrows (*Dance Dance Revolution*) or creating an alternative life (*Second Life* or *Eve*). For many, video gaming is a lot more fulfilling than going to school, working an after-school job, spending time with family, or even obeying the law.

This last one became evident during the crime spree at the release of PlayStation3, which included three UPS workers who stole more than $19,000 worth of the systems during shipment.[6]

Yet what happens when I'm more into my video games than my job? Who'll make the money I need to support my hobby? Or what happens when my wife feels like I love my machine more than I love her? How do I remember it's just a game?

Keep this video-game world in the back of your mind, and let's get a bird's eye view of the kinds of worlds we live in.

Besides video games, humans have created worlds or *diversions* as part of everyday life—diversions their creators hope will make them feel important, valuable, or perceived as being aware. Or people may turn to even deeper diversions that help them dodge life because they don't have any hope or because they have a need for belonging, security, or love.

Our motivations often reveal if something is just a diversion. And the opportunity for diversion is everywhere. The following are just a few of them:

[6] "Three Booked in PlayStation 3 Thefts," *The Times-Picayune* (on www.NOLA.com), December 21, 2006.

DIVERSION #1: MONEY

Many people are controlled by the diversion of making money. To them, money means more spending power.

Others pursue money because it provides material power, and they believe that's true security because it prevents others from taking advantage of them.

Money also helps pretenders believe they're more important than and superior to others.

What motivates the kind of career we want? Is it the amount of money it provides? Or does the job we want match our best abilities?

DIVERSION #2: TRENDS

Some divert to trends, particularly fashion. We want to be perceived as being "aware" and "up-to-date" and "relevant." We desire to belong.

Have you ever thought about what really makes clothing *fashionable*? It changes all the time. I've often wondered what aliens might have thought if they'd landed on our planet back in the '80s and seen our clothing styles. Would they have believed we're intelligent life forms?

I often think we allow fashion to play Jedi Mind Tricks on us.

In *Star Wars Episode IV: A New Hope*, Obi-Wan (Ben) Kenobi and Luke are smuggling droids into the Mos Eisley Spaceport on Tatooine. The stormtroopers interrogate them, but Ben sweeps his hand and uses the Force to control their minds.

Ben: (sweeping his hand) *These aren't the droids you're looking for.*

Stormtrooper: *These aren't the droids we're looking for.*

Ben: (sweeping his hand again) *Move along.*

Stormtrooper: *Move along. Move along.*

Fashion does something similar to us. In the 1990s, the two most popular fashion trendsetters were Madonna and Princess Diana. If they wore it, then "relevant" people followed it. Today, based on what we find in popular magazines, other celebrities now fill those trendsetting roles.

We look to them, and we imitate them. As fashion copycats, we dress up in the latest fashions to show others that we're aware of what's "really" going on. Some will even contradict the popular glamor style with a counter-culture style. That group will play the same fashion games to show they're the smart ones who know what's "really" going on. Our deep desire to be included and part of something important is sewn up in our fashion sense.

And because clothing companies know all about our desire to fit in and our willingness to imitate, they turn on their Jedi Marketing Mind Tricks to prey on us.

Messages flash before us: *Nothing to wear? Come to Merino Outlets. Everything on sale!*

Us: *I'm cleaning out my closet to make room for my new clothes. I must have them. I'm aware of celebrity fashion, and I should be wearing those styles to fit in. Here's my money.*

Messages: *Now you're acceptable. Now you're included. Move along.*

Us: *Now I'm acceptable. Now I'm included. Moving along.*

Fashion mind tricks are multifaceted, and we're vulnerable to them because we believe fashion will give us what we're really looking for. First, celebrities and designers create new designs, and then the marketers promote these latest styles in print, on television, and online to change our tastes toward the new trend.

Then retailers get more of our money, which was all spent on clothes we didn't even need and wouldn't have wanted if we weren't so emotionally needy.[7]

When I was in my early teenage years, I remember how important it was to "peg" my pants. If I didn't do it, people would laugh. Making sure my pants were rolled was more important to me than my homework. I laughed at my parents for taking bell-bottoms so seriously when they were younger. And the cycle of fashion keeps spinning, and we think it's so important.

[7] I suggest you watch *The Merchants of Cool* by Douglas Rushkoff, a documentary on advertising to teenagers. You can see it free at http://www.pbs.org/wgbh/pages/frontline/shows/cool/

Here's a thought about fashion: It has less to do with truth and more to do with trends.

How weird would it be to say skinny pants are *truer* than boot-cut pants? Or bald is *truer* than a mullet? Or stripes are *truer* than plaids?

Yet by looking at the magazine covers displayed by the checkouts in grocery stores, we'd believe fashion is the only remedy to our need to fit in.

And most of us know what happens when we rebel against the opinion of the mob. We feel behind the times, old school, or "*sooo* last year's model." We feel as though we don't belong.

I enjoy fashion, but its overemphasis gets a little weird. Even in a world where people say "everything is relative" and "what's true for you isn't true for me," we still feel pressure to fashionably conform or be left behind. It shows how desperate we are to make sure people think well of us.

Want to know to what degree you seek fashion as a diversion? Ask yourself how much time and money you spend on it. If you don't come from a wealthy family but still insist on carrying a Louis Vuitton bag or buying $100 Nike shoes, for instance, then you're probably seeking fashion as a diversion.

DIVERSION #3: WATERING DOWN GOD

Another diversion is found in our talk about "religion." We divert into passivism to avoid conflict. And avoiding conflict, in our minds, equals peace. But peace is more than the absence of disagreement.

That's because our publicly funded schools insist God is a *religious* idea. Many believe that learning about God isn't truly possible, helpful, or educational. They divert conflict by silencing those conversations, saying talk about God has no bearing on real matters of learning.

Yet when we get on the Internet or watch TV, this idea is taken to the other extreme. Rather than keeping God-talk off-limits, MTV, for instance, creates religious commercials. In 2005, MTV created 24 different "Spiritual Windows" highlighting the religions of the world.[8] With so many different views of God—or gods, really—all being treated as though they're basically the same, how are we supposed to take one view seriously? If all religions are special, then no religion is special.

---

[8] *Chicago Sun-Times*, "MTV's 'Spiritual Windows' Mix Faith with Rock 'n' Roll," March 11, 2005.

The diversion is either to avoid God or to make all gods the same. But real talk—about which God exists, what God is like, and how we can find him—is avoided.

Do you find yourself saying all religions are basically the same? Do you find that talk about God makes you uncomfortable and even stirs up feelings of anger inside you? Do you hate it when people start talking as if more than one God may exist? Pay attention to those feelings and ideas. They may clue you in to the fact that avoiding an honest talk about God is a diversion for you.

DIVERSION #4: OUR PLACES OF WORSHIP

The major trend toward an increased interest in spirituality suggests a diversion.

People turn to Christianity or Islam or Buddhism or Wicca not because they find them true, but because they find them helpful. Or they say it's good for their children to be exposed to moral teaching. Or they find their religion of choice gives them a sense of purpose. All the while, they insist that each of us needs to find the religion that's *right* for us. Rarely do I hear people speak of a religion that's right for everyone without some kind of protest about proselytizing or bigotry.

Even in Christianity I see people attending worship services and finding diversions in the music, their acts of service, their attendance record, and their small groups. So while churchgoers may claim they're trying to have a "God experience," all the while they're simply having a "music experience" that stirs their emotions in a certain way.

Just like all diversions, any of these church activities can be good or bad. What we must question and explore what is our motivation.

DIVERSION #5: OUR MUSIC

We've found music as an endless background noise to fill our lives: Work, study, and free time.

In the ears of students on campuses everywhere, we'll find those famous white earbuds. My sister-in-law has commented that during breaks at her public high school, most students will listen to their music more than they'll talk to other people. I see kids who are willing to hang with their families as long as they can also wear their headphones. They keep themselves plugged in to their music and tuned out to their families.

Music is a tireless diversion today. We play it when we're walking, jogging, driving, resting, studying, partying, and—for some—even sleeping.

Music helps us find a place to belong because, like fashion, we identify with the artists. They give us permission to plant our flag and say, "This is my group. These people understand me." It's an easy way for us to join a side, whether or not that singer or band even cares about us. And it only costs a few bucks.

Another diversion music provides for us is that it moves our emotions. We listen to music to feel *normal*. We also divert some of the other emotions we're feeling—overlaying one emotion with another—by drowning in our music.

A sense of boredom can turn to anger with the push of a play button. Adrenaline pushes through our blood just by skipping ahead to a faster song. And for those few minutes of a song, we can ignore our present situations. And we fear the quiet.

Experts tell us that when we listen to so many other voices through our noise machines, we hardly have time to listen to our own.[9] We don't even know what our own thoughts and beliefs are.

More than meth, marijuana, or alcohol, music today is *the* drug of choice. We need it. Crave it. Feel lost without it.

DIVERSION #6: OUR BUSY SCHEDULES

We have schedules to keep, too: Sports practices, band practices, after-school clubs, friends, television, games, recreational drugs, IMing, chat rooms, and Web surfing, to name but a few.

No wonder students tell me they have no time to live with questions—they're too busy. They say it with enthusiastic insistence—as if being *busy* should be excused at all costs. Busyness becomes a diversion.

It exhausts me to be stuck in busyness, pressured to conform and perform—or get left behind.

---

[9] *Wall Street Journal*, "How to Unplug Your Kids," October 27, 2005.

I received an e-mail from a student who told me he walked away from God because he didn't want to be a hypocrite.

God will understand, he said.

He said he's open to believing in God again, only he didn't have time to really know God because he's too busy with other activities.

God will go easy on me, he said.

For this student, God must be willing to wait on us and excuse our diversions. God must find ways to adapt to *our* lifestyles, fashions, and schedules, or else God will also get left behind.

A SIGN THAT WE "NEED" DIVERSIONS

When we slow down, a certain uneasiness appears to let us know we treasure diversions. *Do we feel a certain uneasy noise in our souls? A discomfort? A certain wiggling to do anything but be still? A nagging feeling that there must be something more?*

Then we ask questions of ourselves (even if we don't voice them)—

Why can't I control my emotions?

How do I stop being angry?

Why am I afraid?

What does God want from me?

Why do I feel insecure around my friends?

Why do I feel so lonely?

But instead of allowing ourselves to ponder and live with these questions, we find something else to take up our thoughts. Maybe we skip tracks to a better song.

It's not a question of whether we have uneasiness or not. We all have it at some level. It's more a question of where we'll go to deal with it.

This will help control my emotions, we think. *This'll take care of the problems I'm sensing in me and around me.*

It will help us *ignore* the uneasiness, anyway.

All of these diversions suffocate our souls because we use them to silence the noise in us and around us.

And we get into the habit of believing the remedy is just a matter of changing our feelings for the moment, and then maybe our loneliness and dissatisfaction will fade. Then the lyric by U2 may become our own: "I still haven't found what I'm looking for."

LOST IN THE WILD

Go with me into J.R.R. Tolkien's *The Lord of the Rings*. Among the vast mountains and marshes of Middle-Earth walk Frodo and Sam, two Hobbits of the Shire. Their quest is to destroy the One Ring.

Tolkien writes that they are "bewildered." At the heart of that word, is another word—*wild*. Tolkien, a linguist, means exactly what he writes. Frodo and Sam are out in the wild, nearly directionless, and carrying a ring they never wanted into a land no Hobbit dared enter. They don't know the way.

We, too, are bewildered. We are in our own version of the Wild. We are born into it, and we find ourselves alone in it. Many people surround us—some who love us, but many who don't—yet nobody really knows us deep down. Nobody completely understands us. We feel alone. We feel lost in the Wild.

To deal with it, we find new diversions—hobbies, music, activities, even religion—anything to keep us from the sad tale that we don't know the way to go.

Yet we want to find our way Home.

OTHER WORLDS

In Frodo's story, the armies of Rohan gather themselves along the largest city of the race of Men. Minas Tirith assembles its sentries on the walls, while Gandalf rides Shadowfax to the inner chambers where the Steward rules that white city. The moving Shadow of Mordor darkens the earth and sky with shadow, the Nazgul, and the Orc armies. The light and freedom of Middle-Earth are at stake.

How strange would it be if a group of rogue Elves sat on a nearby hilltop smoking and holding signs that say, *War is not the answer!*

Yet this is our world in the Wild. Many people are more willing to let our souls dwindle than to say something is wrong with the Shadows that surround us.

I long to exist in a world—even if for only a few minutes—where it's not about more shopping, music, and busy schedules. I desire to live in a world full of purpose and to find a village worth saving.

I want a place where I matter.

I may need to be like Bilbo Baggins, putting aside my walking stick and strapping on a sword so I can confront the dragon.

I have to agree with that Mountain Dew banner: *Protecting your village from the dragon is way more important than your job.*

Our village is Home, and our quest is to get there. It's where we want to live, be at peace, and be ourselves. Home is partly our community when we put down the selfish, dishonest, and fearful masks and get honest. Protecting our community, our nation, our world, and our lives will always be more important than our jobs.

Yet, how will we survive? We all desire to belong, to take part in fulfilling work, to experience deep relationships, and to be safe with a stable family. How will we accomplish this?

Throw more money at fashion so we'll look like everyone else? Throw ourselves into casual sexual encounters in an effort to find intimacy? Throw ourselves into an endless cycle of online gaming? Throw more hours into work we may not even believe in, just because we want to own a nicer car or appear more capable?

These are all legitimate desires. Yet if we don't live with life's deeper questions, then as we stare these desires in the eye, we'll find ourselves following them as simple diversions, instead of seeing them as a small part of something much bigger.

We don't have to fulfill our desires purely for the sake of endless entertainment or to avoid the deeper questions. We can step beyond the Jedi Mind Tricks and start asking questions.

Questions that will help us be ourselves.

MEANING BEHIND THE NOISE?

Behind all the noise in our world, life was originally supposed to be meaningful. All the fashion, popular music, and diversions are just a flashy tinfoil that covers what we long for most.

Could it be that the world we were born into has forgotten something important? Are we hiding in the Wild with a need to get Home?

We want a sense of adventure and purpose.
We want goodness to reign and evil to be destroyed.
We want to belong.
We long to count or matter to someone.
But we don't want to be lost.

What if one of our goals in life were to say we will follow our questions through the Wild wherever they lead us? What if we no longer needed life's diversions? Perhaps just over another hill or around another hedge, we'll find a purpose to life more beautiful, more sacred, and more terrible than we ever imagined.

THE QUESTION

"Does it matter what I think as long as I'm having fun?" a student asked me, a teasing smile on her face.

She knows there's something missing, yet she wants to do something truly satisfying.

But it may also mean she needs to stop fiddling with life in the Wild, stop feeding herself with diversions, and get knee-deep into what it's really all about.

"Does it matter what I think as long as I'm having fun?"

What she's really saying is,

Come on! Does my mind really matter? Does the hard work of sifting through ideas really pay off? Please don't pester me with what I believe or what you believe and let's just enjoy a fun, easy life!

As an explorer living with questions, she's planted her flag in the soil of thought and raised it high with her question: *Does it matter what I think?*

THINKING MATTERS

When I was arrested with my friends on that Halloween night, a cold cup of ideas splashed in my face. They shocked and scared me. Up to that time, I was holding the wrong ideas about my purpose in life. I'd just assumed they were the right ideas, without really thinking about them.

I was basically standing in the dark, believing it was the light, until the real light shone in.

Ideas...

• are what we think about.

• may even be things we just assume and don't ever think about.

• determine the kind of person we'll marry.

• determine where we'll go to college.

• determine how much we value relationships and which friends we select.

• determine how much time we spend with our noses in front of a television

> or in a book

>> or in front of a mirror putting on makeup every morning or getting our hair just right,

> or practicing athletics, musical instruments, algebra, photography, or anything else we put our hands to.

• control our emotions much of the time.

• tell us how much our emotions, in turn, are allowed to control us.

• govern and can actually alter our desires in different directions—for good and bad.

• can either brainwash us into being slaves or shape us into leaders.

Ideas will ultimately determine the kind of people we'll become. Ideas are no small thing.

IDEAS THAT SHAPED A DANGEROUS CAUSE

In the 1920s, there was an eloquent young man whom people loved to listen to when he spoke at political rallies. On one occasion, he led his political party to revolt and was then sentenced to a year in prison. During his time in jail, he reflected on the revolt, on his politics, and on his country. He even began to pen his ideas in a journal, and eventually he formed a book he titled *My Struggle*. After he was released from prison, he published his book, and it captured the imaginations of his fellow countrymen.

The German name of this book is *Mein Kampf*, and the name of the book's author is Adolf Hitler. As you know, Hitler is recorded as being among the most evil dictators of all time.

Among Hitler's ideas: He believed his fellow Germans and other white people were superior to other races, such as Jews and Africans. He also held an *idea* that the Jewish race was more closely related to animals than to people. He said that like wolves, "Jews stand together in the plundering of their fellow men." He claimed that the devil himself, as "the symbol of all evil, assumes the living shape of the Jew."[10]

So Hitler had the Jews exterminated.

More than six million Jewish people died in the early 1940s under Hitler's Nazi regime—all because of *ideas*. Hitler thought Germany should reign through a violent assault on the rest of Europe and the world. His military machinery killed millions during World War II, all because of a few quiet *ideas* that were penned from within the silence of a jail cell in the middle of Europe.

---

[10] Adolf Hitler, *Mein Kampf*, Volume One, Chapter XI, Nation and Race.

WHAT ARE YOUR IDEAS *ABOUT* IDEAS?

Right now, sit quietly for a moment and consider whether or not ideas even matter to you.

If they don't, then there's no reason to ask whether you have the right ideas or not.

If they don't matter, then your idea that "ideas don't matter" doesn't really matter either.

If you think about it longer, that conclusion is self-deception in the name of laziness or selfishness. Or, even more, to say "ideas don't matter" may be the verbal equivalent of lifting your middle finger and demanding to be left alone.

Disregarding the power of ideas is like driving on the interstate with your eyes closed. At some point, reality won't care if you believe in it or not. It will present itself to you in the form of a guardrail or an oncoming train or cliff.

And, bewildered, you'll be falling fast.

Or, like me, you may find yourself in the hands of the police, wondering what happened.

If ideas don't matter to you, then expect your life to ultimately follow a winding, messy path, leaving you adrift in the Wild from the things that matter most.

And if your life becomes a disaster, you'll feel regret like

- a sea captain who's shipwrecked because the *idea* of a compass didn't matter.

 - the mother of a dead child because the *idea* that seatbelts save lives didn't matter.

  - a homeowner after a burglary because the *idea* that locks protect us didn't matter.

If ideas don't matter, then ultimately *life* doesn't matter.

We'd end up with no more purpose than the animals. Enslaved by our instincts and passions, we'd give no thought to wisdom or foolishness, and we'd ignore the past and not plan for the future. In the end, we'd be whisked away to do someone else's bidding.

All the people we admire most—from Michelangelo to Thomas Edison, from George Washington to Thomas Jefferson, from Mother Teresa to Socrates, from Gandhi to Wilberforce, from Martin Luther King to Jesus Christ—all believed in the power of ideas. Although they didn't necessarily agree on which ideas mattered most, they all agreed that ideas do matter.

CHILDLIKE FAITH?

If you're not yet convinced, let's see what God thinks about ideas. Do they matter to God?

I was recently giving a presentation at a church. The music was well chosen. The people cheerfully and seriously praised God. And then the pastor prayed, "Lord, give us childlike ignorance because we know we can never understand you."

Childlike ignorance? What? Whoa! I thought. *Is that our fear of living with questions talking?*

Many people in the Wild believe we cannot know or understand God. Because of this, they believe that knowing God doesn't matter.

Did this pastor have God all wrong?

One thing is for sure: God doesn't want us to remain children forever. God wants us to grow up, relish life and responsibility, learn, love, and know him better. Yet many times we're told "don't take life so seriously" or even "you should have a childlike ignorance." As I questioned things during my teenage years, many nice adults said, "Stop thinking so much" and "Take it by faith."

A verse that's often quoted in the church to squelch questioners is found in Matthew 18. People will sometimes use it to say we should have "childlike faith," which really means "childlike ignorance." Let's look at the passage:

At that time the disciples came to Jesus and asked, "Who, then, is the greatest in the kingdom of heaven?"

He called a little child, whom he placed among them. And he said: "Truly I tell you, unless you change and become like little children, you will never enter the kingdom of heaven. Therefore, whoever takes a humble place—becoming like this child—is the greatest in the kingdom of heaven." (Matthew 18:1-4)

Here's the scene: The closest students of Jesus wonder which of them will be the greatest in the kingdom of heaven. Obviously, they were into honor, prestige, and comparing themselves to one another. The problem of *pride* is as ancient as it is modern. So Jesus pulls aside a child and says to his followers that unless they become like that youngster, they cannot get into the kingdom of heaven.

What did Jesus mean? How are we supposed to become like children?

If we take Jesus' statement out of context and simply say, "Unless you become like children…" then we can arrive at many silly conclusions:

Should we become *ignorant* like children?

Should we *smear hot fudge on ourselves* when we eat sundaes?

Should we *pick our noses*?

Should we *bounce on grandpa's knee* to attain the kingdom of God?

Are these the keys to gaining entrance into God's kingdom? Is this what Jesus was talking about?

When we make this verse say *anything* that pertains to children—even childlike ignorance—it's absurd.

Fortunately, we don't have to guess what Jesus meant; we just have to keep reading.

This is called putting things in *context*. I already mentioned the scene: The disciples are asking Jesus a question. Jesus makes his remark about becoming like a child. We must keep reading to understand what Jesus means. "*Therefore, whoever takes a humble place—becoming like this child…*"

Jesus is clear and precise. Do you see the virtue Jesus speaks of? It's not *ignorance*. It's *humility*. Children are humble. They know they need help tying their shoes or reaching for the cereal. They have no pride in needing Mommy and Daddy to protect them. They're aware they need someone bigger than themselves—such as their parents and even God.

Brennan Manning put it this way: "For the disciple of Jesus 'becoming like a little child' means the willingness to accept oneself as being of little account and to be regarded as unimportant"[11] and, I might add, regarding God as ultimately important. What does this tell us? Jesus does not want us to be ignorant, stupid, or harmless. Rather, *humility* is the key to the kingdom of heaven. In fact, it's the key to our finding things good, true, and beautiful. And asking questions and searching for ideas that are true is one way to grow in humility.

GOD'S CONCERN FOR OUR IDEAS

Is it possible that the God of all reason created us to be unreasonable?

God isn't against thinking. God thinks, just as we should think. In fact, God gave us the ability to do so and is quite insistent that we fill our minds with great ideas.

Paul refers to this in Romans 12:2:

Do not conform to the pattern of this world, but be transformed by the renewing of your mind. Then you will be able to test and approve what God's will is—his good, pleasing and perfect will.

Notice that Paul doesn't say our minds should be removed, but *renewed!* The Master of the Universe tells us to use our minds to navigate the Wild. This is one reason why Paul says, "And do not conform to the pattern of this world." In other words, "Don't be a slave to the creative diversions of the masses and of our own making."

God is telling us to open our minds. God wants us to reach out and grab great ideas, harness them, take them into our souls, and live them as full-blooded human beings. To bend our minds away from the Wild and toward the warm hearth of Home.

Great ideas are not for the closed-minded but for those who are ready for the challenge. In fact, God wants us to employ our minds to think the most rigorous thoughts—specifically about God's character, power, and good and perfect will. In short, God wants us to understand his mind, purposes, and way of thinking and doing things. This cannot be done if we pursue "childlike ignorance."

Now does this mean we can know *all* of God's thoughts? Clearly, no. But we can know enough of them to fill our minds with goodness and

[11] Brennan Manning, *The Ragamuffin Gospel.*

expand our imaginations to limits far beyond our video-gaming worlds.

Ideas matter to God. He framed the world with them. And God wants great ideas to roll around in our minds the way they roll around in his. This includes ideas all throughout the Bible, as well as our everyday interests—art, science, philosophy, relationships, sports, and entertainment. God desires for us to navigate all of these areas—not as sniveling weaklings who are pulled about by diversion, but as healthy, confident, and attractive souls.

THE DRAGON

Long before the race of Humans came into the world, there was a mighty angel—great in both rank and honor—serving in the high court of God. Though we know few details, we do know this angel wanted a station higher than the one he was created to possess. He wanted God's place, God's throne, God's power.

And with that, God struck him down. The angel wasn't built to be God; if he wouldn't choose what he was created to be, then he'd become far less.

His angelic name was Lucifer, the light bringer. Today, he's known as Satan, and he's no storybook creature with horns and a pitchfork. Even depictions of him in movies such as the *Exorcist* hardly match his twistedness.

In Revelation 12:9, he's called, "the great dragon." Satan is smart and savvy. He has more power than the world's empires combined, yet he can subtly influence the hearts of men and women with prettiness, pleasure, and half-truths.

He is active in the Wild, and he desires to devour people to fill his house below. Satan is a mastermind who strategizes with his Jedi Mind Tricks on how best to capture the weak.

Why doesn't God just crush this horrible creature? If God has so much power, why doesn't God simply wipe out Satan altogether? Well, God could, and God will—one day. But not yet. The battle is not between God and Satan. The battle is over what *we* will do with our ideas about God.

There is a battle between Heaven and Hell over whether God is good. And the battle is for the human heart.[12]

God could crush Satan in an instant. Yet that's not in God's purposes right now. God is more concerned about us. Will we see God as good? Will we choose to be God's friend? Or will we pretend we are God? Will we tell God to buzz off? Satan may influence us in many directions, but we still have the freedom to pursue God—or not.

Here's what the Bible says about the battle against the Dragon:

The weapons we fight with are not the weapons of the world. On the contrary, they have divine power to demolish strongholds. We demolish arguments and every pretension that sets itself up against the knowledge of God, and we take captive every thought to make it obedient to Christ. (2 Corinthians 10:4, 5)

The Dragon's major strategy is not swinging his mighty tail or enflaming our villages with fire. Rather, Satan works to make us believe that ideas don't matter. He wants us to lack understanding about the Wild and the way Home. He wants us distracted and ignorant. He wants us apathetic. He wants us plugged into our electronics and listening to a multitude of other voices so we hardly know our own. In other words, he wants us to trust our diversions.

The Enemy isn't interested in getting us to disbelieve God or to become atheists. That's not an effective strategy for him because thoughtful atheists are still at risk of thinking hard about God.

No, the Enemy has something more sinister in mind.

At the heart of Satan's warfare is his ongoing plan for us to misunderstand or disregard who God is and what God is like. It's an attack on our *knowledge* of God. So he effectively uses our diversions, which lead us to search for fulfillment in the things that don't—and can't—fulfill us, until we end up ignoring our souls' true satisfactions. Satan wants us playing in the Wild among the marshes of the dead, rather than looking for road signs that will lead us to safety. And he knows that if we misunderstand God or find God irrelevant, we'll misunderstand the importance of everything else as well.

But who will take up arms against him?

---

[12] Paraphrase from a discussion on beauty in Fyodor Dostoevsky's, *The Brothers Karamazov*.

One of my favorite writers once said, "It is not that we have not got enough scoundrels to curse, but that we have not got enough good men to curse them."[13] Our Home needs protecting from the many bad ideas that the Dragon flames down upon us. Many of us get burned, yet we don't even know it. We're just out in the fields, wearing our headphones and dancing with our eyes closed.

But there is one essential starting point to protect us, which, if we don't get it right, little else will help us win the fight. It's not more prayer, although more prayer is necessary. It's not more Bible study, although that's good, too. It's not spending more time at church, although that will help us band together with other believers in the task. Rather, our protection is to arm ourselves with the best ideas we can find and then walk in them.[14]

Facing ideas, weeding through them, and using new tools along the way will help us understand ourselves, our hurts, our struggles, and how to deal with them without turning to easy diversions. This is no battle of swords and bombs.

This is a battle for our minds. What I think matters. And what *you* think matters.

QUESTIONS TO LIVE INTO

Find a place where you can have 15 minutes alone in the quiet (that means turning off music, TV, cell phone, etc.). Ask yourself these questions:

If all jobs paid $10 per hour, what job would you choose? Why?

When you feel uneasy, lost, lonely, afraid, be-*wild*-ered what do you do? How often do you use the following as diversions?

Money-seeking

Fashion

[13] "Public Confessions by Politicians," *Illustrated London News*, 1908-1910, vol. 28 of *The Collected Works of G.K. Chesterton*, ed. George Marlin and Lawrence Clipper (San Francisco: Ignatius Press, 1987), 64. Quoted in *Permanent Things*, ed. Andrew A. Tadie and Michael H. Macdonald (Grand Rapids, Mich.: Eerdmans, 1995), 30.

[14] Ephesians 6:10-20.

Church

Music

Busyness

What other diversions do you use that aren't on this list?

Why do you feel drawn to certain diversions? What do they do for you?

Unplug. Try going one day without listening to music. Any music. Then write down how you felt when you wanted to listen to music as your diversion. Were you surprised? Do you find it hard to admit how you really feel about this? After you go one day without music, next time try a whole weekend. After that, try a whole week. See what happens.

Find a friend and ask, "Do you think about your purpose in life?" See what happens. If your friend says *yes,* follow it up with, "Does it change how you think about life?" Discuss that a bit.

Hunt for Jedi Mind Tricks. Watch your favorite TV show. Pay close attention to the commercials. Whom are they trying to convince? What are advertisers trying to get you to believe? Do you find it easy to believe what they're telling you? Do you find you suddenly have new "needs" that you didn't have before you watched the commercial? Does the commercial change what you buy?

NOTES

_____

_____

_____

_____

_____

_____

_____

_____

_____

_____

_____

_____

_____

_____

_____

_____

_____

_____

_____

_____

_____

_____

_____

QUESTION 2

WHAT IS *TRUTH?*

DEFINE *TRUTH*

Before we begin this part of the book, I want you to do something first. Right here in the space provided—and without looking ahead—write down your definition of *truth*. Don't worry; you won't be graded. It's a definition just for you, to help you compare your understanding of *truth* now and what you will have at the end of this chapter. You may be surprised.

So what is *truth*? Define it.

(Don't just stare at the white space. I'm not watching. Go ahead—write something down. Come on, don't be shy. Take a stab at it!)

_____

_____

_____

Okay, let's go.

In an episode of *The Simpsons* entitled "She of Little Faith," Lisa embarks on a spiritual quest. While talking to Bart, Lisa says she's seeking "a religion that is right for me." She eventually discovers Buddhism and learns she can worship with any kind of religion as long as it promotes love. Satisfied, Lisa returns home to celebrate Christmas with her family. And as long as Lisa still participates in the family's Christian rituals, Homer is satisfied as well.

I usually enjoy watching *The Simpsons* because it holds up a mirror to our culture and asks us to reflect on who we are and what we've become. And I'm afraid the writers are correct in their assessments of how Christianity is perceived in our culture.

When Lisa says, "To find a religion that is right for me," the scriptwriters have made religion into something that can be dropped into a shopping cart.[15] Religion here isn't a belief system that could be true or false—it's an accessory, like looking for the hat that's "just right for me." In trying to

---

[15] I believe a shopping cart is a good picture of the way people today treat religion in the Wild. We treat each other as consumers with many options of things to buy—lipstick, cookies, socks, coat hangers, chocolate, and, while we're at it, let's put some religion in the shopping buggy. It'll accessorize me. It'll make me feel more confident about myself. Except that religion doesn't fit into a shopping cart. Religious *activities* might, but *religion* doesn't. Religion says a certain set of claims are true, and that if you live according to those claims, you'll find your purpose. And every religion has a different set of claims.

compliment all religions by saying they're basically the same, *The Simpsons* insulted every religion by implying none of them are unique.

Yet, I think I may agree with Lisa—just in a different way. I believe we do need to find the religion that's right for us, just like I need to find the medicine that's right for my bronchitis. I'm not looking for a religion that merely sounds pretty or makes me look better. Nor am I looking for the cough syrup that tastes like roasted almonds but can't clear up the congestion in my lungs. I'm looking for the religion (and the cough syrup) that deals with truth—right down to the core.

If we find this religion, this *true* religion, then it will be right for everyone, including Lisa Simpson. On the other hand, a false religion is right for no one, just like bad medicine is right for no one.

No one benefits in the long term by ignoring the way life is and the design of the universe. No one benefits by praying to gods who don't exist. No matter how much we might believe in the Easter Bunny, hoping and praying won't make it come hopping into our lives.

We need a religion that, as one writer put it, is "right where we are right" and "right where we are wrong."[16]

Today, *truth* is in need of a friend. In politics, *truth* is what the voters vote for. In Hollywood, *truth* is what moviegoers pay for. In fashion, *truth* is whatever the trend is. In food, *truth* is whatever suits your tastes.

But what about *truth* itself?

In mathematics, some school curriculums are telling us we can no longer depend on the "truth" about numbers—2 + 2 may now equal 7.[17]

In morality, "truth" becomes whatever an individual or group decides is right for them. In other words, truth isn't discovered—it's invented.

People then confuse the laws in our society with morality. Since laws are created, they believe morality is created. They forget that people start with morality and make laws to *guard* that morality.

They forget things can be immoral but legal—such as the way slavery was immoral but legal many years ago. Or the way some view abortion as immoral but legal.

Things can also be illegal but not immoral, too, such as jaywalking.

[16] G.K. Chesterton, *The Catholic Church and Conversion.*
[17] Nancy Pearcey, *Total Truth.*

WHERE HAS TRUTH GONE?

A famous journalist of the 20th century once reported how truth was ignored in the Russian Kremlin when it was run by communist leaders. As the proposals were shared, one man raised his hand and said, "But if we tell the people this, it wouldn't be true."

An awkward silence rolled through the room. Then one man began to chuckle. Then another. And another. Until soon the whole assembly was laughing until tears ran down their cheeks.

You see, when a society turns godless, some person or group of persons or even *every* person becomes a little god in the process, and they start making up their own rules. But as this journalist pointed out, that moment in the Kremlin revealed the bankruptcy of the people. "It is truth that has died, not God."[18]

When truth dies, the rails on which to run our lives are removed. Without truth, we cannot know things. Without the ability to know things, we cannot use things properly. If we cannot use things properly, we cannot take care of things properly.

After I bought my Jeep, the first thing I wanted to do was remove the hard top and put on the soft top. Some of my friends came over, and we pored over the directions in the manual. A half hour later, our work was done. But first we had to take the time to understand how the top on the Jeep worked before we could make it do what it was designed to do. We needed the *truth*.

One philosopher said, "What you would take care of you must first understand, whether it be a petunia or a nation."[19]

But what about taking care of ourselves? Do we believe truth exists? Let's look at a survey of students ages 13 to 18. The survey asked a wide array of questions about topics from music to religion. The questions were organized, in part, to answer a bigger question, "Do you believe in absolute truth?" What would you answer?

---

[18] Malcolm Muggeridge, Chronicles of Wasted Time: The Green Stick.
[19] Dallas Willard, Renovation of the Heart.

Knowing your friends from school, clubs, and the neighborhood, what percentage do you think would say there really is such a thing as absolute truth? When you have a percentage in your head, turn the page.

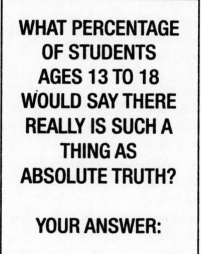

WHAT PERCENTAGE OF STUDENTS AGES 13 TO 18 WOULD SAY THERE REALLY IS SUCH A THING AS ABSOLUTE TRUTH?

YOUR ANSWER:

_____

According to the national survey, only **nine percent** of all young people, religious and non-religious, affirm there is such a thing as absolute truth.[20]

Does that surprise you? Or did you expect the percentage to be that low?[21]

Interestingly, only a small percentage of students denied there was absolute truth. Most students were in the middle, neither affirming nor denying the existence of absolute truth.[22] There's a good chance you also fit into this middle category.

When I speak to teenagers, I hear this question, "What is *truth*?" These are brave students, and they encourage me. They're asking one of the great questions of our time.

Some people say today's students don't care about truth, and they just want to do whatever feels good. But I don't believe that. I don't see that on the street. When students say such things, they're either lying, or they're contradicting the way they live, or as one professor says, they're just trying to end the conversation.[23]

I believe students care about being good friends and performing well in sports, hobbies, or music. And all of these things require truth to do them well. So why the low percentage—why only nine percent?

Could it possibly be because most students don't even know what *absolute truth* is?

To many, truth is an alien concept, such as stating that bibliokleptomania[24] is a fungus.

WHAT IS ABSOLUTE TRUTH?

In formal discussion groups with students, I've asked them to define *absolute truth* as a group. I approach the whiteboard with marker in hand, ready to scribble down their profound answers.

"What," I ask, "is *absolute truth*?"

---

[20] In this chapter, the terms *absolute truth* and *truth* will be used interchangeably.
[21] Interestingly, when I ask groups of teenagers this question, far more than nine percent of them raise their hands.
[22] George Barna, *Real Teens: A Contemporary Snapshot of Youth Culture.*
[23] Michael P. Lynch, *True to Life: Why Truth Matters.*
[24] *Bibliokleptomania* is actually the compulsive desire to steal books. It's particularly hated by librarians.

"When you think that…um, when…" This student's thought trails off, and he looks at the ceiling with a sigh.

"Reality."

"What you like."

"What you believe."

Then I turn to the adults in the group and ask the same question. One leader remarks, "When what you think is true?"

Oops. We can't use the word we're defining as part of the definition. That's like defining *sailing* as, er, "to sail."

I've had adult leaders approach me and admit that students don't know how to define *truth* because their teachers don't know much about it, either.

I hope you feel a bit relieved by that. It's hard to believe in something if you don't even know what it is. It may not be your fault.

But you're still responsible to know what it is.

I'm confident that most teachers *affirm* absolute truth, even though they can't define it. They have a sense of what it is; however, that sense is not often clear enough to pass on to the next generation—your generation. Is there any wonder why students today don't know how to answer the question of whether or not there is absolute truth? We simply don't know what it is.

The definition of *truth* is quite simple, but it takes some thinking. Like the rules of tennis, truth is simple to understand. But you have to pay attention to start getting it. And no matter who you are, whether you're an A student or a D student, you can understand this and use it in your everyday world:

Truth is an idea or a belief about something that shows up in the real world.

Or to put it another way, *truth is when an idea reflects the way the world really is.*

Or to put it another way, *truth is an idea or a belief that is a fact.*

Or more philosophically speaking—*truth is a proposition that corresponds to reality.*

Whew, there's the definition! All of these say pretty much the same thing, just in different ways. Now reread these definitions to make sure you've got it in your head.

TRUTH EXAMPLES

Suppose I'm looking for my car keys. I usually have a hard time putting them in the same place twice. My wife, Jonalyn, set up a system in our home where the keys go in the key box near the door. But I keep forgetting about that system, and I only remember it when my keys are lost.

So I'm still looking for my car keys.

Upon walking into my study, I suddenly see the keys sitting on my desk. I *see* the keys. I now have the *idea* that the keys are sitting on the desk. Because the idea that the keys are sitting on the desk accurately reflects the *fact* that the keys are on the desk, I now have *truth*. My idea mirrors the way things are. My idea links with the facts, just as a rock climber links his carabiner with the piton drilled into the side of the mountain.

Suppose I'm planning to drive to Gino's Pizza in Laguna Beach. Unsure of where the restaurant is located, I go online and print out the directions. Then I follow every turn, and I arrive at the pizza place precisely as the map directs me. The map was true because the map reflects the way the roads *really* are.

Many times, however, those online maps have led me astray, and I've had to stop at gas stations to ask for the proper directions. In those moments, we'd probably call the map *false*. Why? Because it does *not* reflect the way the roads *really* are. (And my friends ate all the pizza because I was late.)

Since we're using the topic of driving, let's suppose my Jeep is in the shop for a flat tire. A few hours pass before I receive a phone call from my mechanic who says the work is complete.

Suddenly, a new idea comes into my mind that I have a repaired tire on my truck. I haven't actually *seen* the tire. I only have the idea of this repaired tire because my mechanic told me about it. My wife drives me to the shop. I pay the bill, take my keys, and go to my Jeep. I look down at the wheel sporting a freshly repaired tire. In that instant, the idea that my tire was repaired corresponds[25] with the *real* repaired tire I'm looking at. In that moment—when my *belief* about the tire and the *real* tire link up together—I experience *truth*.

Here's a diagram to think about:

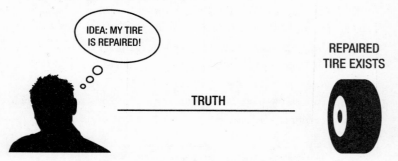

Truth is all about the content of ideas linking with the way the world is.

If this still isn't clear, go back a few paragraphs, read the examples again, and see if it doesn't make a little more sense to you.[26]

The goal of this chapter (like all important things) is not for us to complete it quickly, but to understand it well. Give yourself the freedom to take your time on it. And always be willing to reread.

TRUTH IN ROMANCE

When Jonalyn first caught my eye, it was because she let her hair down—literally. She usually hid those beautiful, thick, brown curls by wearing her hair up. But one evening she let her hair down, and it caught my attention. That's when I started talking with her more and sending e-mails to her.

---

[25] There are a few theories about truth that work together. The view of truth I'm talking about here is called the *Correspondence Theory of Truth.* It's the oldest view of truth and has been believed throughout history by a variety of philosophers such as Aristotle, an Augustine. (If you're more philosophically minded, here's some more information to consider: *Correspondence Theory* basically says that truth is a proposition that "corresponds" to reality. A *proposition* is the content of a sentence.)

[26] Or if it still doesn't make sense after reading over it a few times, go online to our Web site (www.soulation.org). We're often chatting online, and we'd be glad to help you some more!

I was getting the impression she liked me, too. I mean, after all, do people keep writing you back and calling you on the phone if they don't?

My belief that she liked me continued to grow, until one day I asked her to be my girlfriend. It took her a couple days to reply (and I felt as though I were dangling on the edge of a cliff), but she finally said *yes*.

In that moment of excitement, something happened (besides sparks flying). *Truth* happened. My *belief* that she liked me linked up with the reality that she did like me. I was a lucky guy.

Truth is everywhere, like the air we breathe. Even in our dating lives.

So let's review here: **Truth** *is when an idea links up with the real world.* Such as those times when I found my keys, realized my tire was repaired, and discovered that my belief that Jonalyn liked me actually reflected the fact that she really did like me.

This definition of *truth* is so important—I cannot stress it enough. Burn the concept into your mind.

BUT...HOW DO WE KNOW?

It drives me nuts when I'm in a conversation with someone who says, "Well, that's just your *opinion*." For some reason, people seem to believe that an *opinion* doesn't count during serious discussions. When people say things like that, I figure they just want me to be quiet. Their tone reveals to me that they wholeheartedly believe that what *they're* sharing is not mere opinion, but actual fact.

However, opinions are beliefs about the facts. Both sides hold opinions because both sides think their beliefs are more closely aligned with the facts. We only hold opinions that we believe are true. So whether we call it a "belief" or an "opinion," it doesn't matter. They mean the same thing.

Here comes the good part: How do we *know* if something is true or not? *Truth* and *knowledge* are different—but related—animals.

Truth is when an idea about something links with the real world. *Knowledge* comes when we have *reasons* for believing an idea links with the real world. Therefore, *knowledge* is dependent upon *reasons.*

And just because something is true doesn't mean we *know* it's true. Long ago, humans believed there were extraterrestrials living on nearby planets. Was it *true*? Mars could have been peopled with green creatures carrying laser guns (if some science-fiction writers are correct). But how would we *know* if that were true or not?

Well, first we invented bigger telescopes, and then we sent two rovers—*Spirit* and *Opportunity*—to explore Mars. Was it *true* that aliens live on Mars? No. Was it *true* that Mars was uninhabited? Yes. How did we *know?* We searched and explored the planet. We now had *reasons* to say we *know* there's no life on Mars. According to all of our information, we have reason to believe it's true that Mars is an uninhabited planet. When we have good reasons for an idea, we call that *knowledge.*

This discipline of using reasons to know we have *truth* is called **epistemology** (a-PIS-te-MOL-o-gie). Epistemology is a field of philosophy that studies reasons for why we know things. Even if we cannot pronounce the word, we use epistemology all day, every day.

I share this strange word with you because I know you can handle it. In school you have to learn the rules of basketball, the parts of the cell, and the American presidents. When I was in fifth grade, my whole class had to learn the countries of Europe and their capitals. Therefore, I believe you can handle a word like *epistemology.*

Now, let's go through some of those general tools that epistemology gives us and apply them to our lives.[27]

FIVE TOOLS FOR KNOWLEDGE

There are five different tools that give us correct understanding so we can know things: *perception, reason, introspection, testimony,* and *memory.* Everything we know comes to us through one or more of these five tools. When we're trying to figure out if something is true, we want to use as many of these access ways as possible. The more of them we have in place, the more confident we are that we *know* the *truth.*

[27] Again, for you philosophy types, my view is called "moderate" or "modest" foundationalism. It's considered the most widely held view among epistemologists today.

1. PERCEPTION

The phrase "Seeing is believing" comes from this first tool of epistemology. What is *perception*? If I say, "I perceive it's snowing," I can mean several things. I can go outside and **see** the snow. I **feel** the snow on my face. I can tilt my head back and **taste** the crystal snow on my tongue. I can **smell** the moisture in the air. If I'm quiet, I can even **hear** it nestling on the leaves.

If we have the idea that "it's snowing," I can know it's true by using my perception (seeing, feeling, tasting, smelling, and hearing) to find out that my idea is backed up by facts. We now *know* it's *true*!

You see, epistemology is practical, especially if you're deciding whether to lie out to get a tan or hit the half-pipe on the slopes that day. The only way you'd *know* is by developing your epistemology. Using your *perception* is part of understanding your epistemology or reasons for belief.

2. REASON

Six is always greater than two. How do you *know*? Well, we need our second tool.

This one doesn't require us to go outside in the snow. In fact, we can use it without leaving the house, our bedroom, or even our own bed on a Saturday morning. It's called *reason.*

When you think of the word *reason*, don't think of your mind. Don't even think of the word *reasonable* yet. Just look at the word *reason* as I give it a more precise definition. Philosophers call it *a priori reason*, so if you ever see it mentioned in other places (and it's being used by more than just philosophers today), you'll know what they're talking about.

What is reason? It's a built-in common sense. It's those conclusions we reach without having to go exploring to do so. Reason comes *prior* to your testing it out (that's where the *a priori* comes in).

If someone were to ask us the question, "Is there such a thing as a circular square snowflake?" we wouldn't have to go outside in a snowstorm before we answered. Nor would we have to sail with Christopher Columbus into unknown seas to figure it out. We already know the answer because of our ability to *reason.*

In our minds, we automatically know that a "circular square" is a contradiction. It's contradictory to say something is circular *and* square at the same time and in the same way. Circles are circles, and they're circular. Squares are squares, and they're boxy. If we attempted to make a circular square snowflake, we'd find it impossible. At best, we'd come up with a different shape altogether, such as a trapezoid. But a trapezoid is neither a square nor a circle.

Notice we didn't need science, a microscope, a telescope, or the daily newspaper to tell us this. We simply used our *reason;* and we *know* the *truth* that contradictions—e.g., square circles—cannot exist.[28] Of course, just as with our other tools, our *reason* isn't perfect. We need to examine other people's reasoning and use our other tools to compare. But reason is still a powerful tool.

3. INTROSPECTION

How much do you enjoy strawberries? Only one human in the whole world can answer that question: you! No one except *you* can say what you enjoy. And that's the purpose of this next tool, and many people don't even realize they have it. It's called *introspection.*

What is introspection? It's access to our inner life. We have the ability to look into ourselves and find out what we're thinking and feeling. Nobody else can describe what we really believe and feel. They may see us pouting with a pudgy lower lip or jumping up and down with excitement. But that's all they can see. They may guess that those gestures mean something is going on inside you, but no one has access to our real thoughts, feelings, intentions, and motivations. Only we can reveal them.

Teachers will tell us, "You need to know your mind!" Or our girl-friend or boyfriend will grin with a leading question, "So, what's on your mind? What'cha thinkin' about?"

Those questions can only be answered with the tool of introspection. We have the ability to figure out what we really believe and only you and God have access to that inner place. No scientist can poke around in your brain and tell if you like strawberries; you're the only one with the privilege of knowing your own thoughts, tastes, desires, and beliefs.

---

[28] Logic also falls under this category of reason. In fact, the logical law I just used is called *The Law of Non-Contradiction.* It says that something cannot have two opposite properties in the same way at the same time.

4. TESTIMONY

What happened on January 5, 2002? I got married. I know it's true because I was there. And now *you* know it because I told you. This is an example of our fourth tool: *Testimony*.

When I use the word *testimony*, don't think of people getting up in church and talking about how their lives changed when they turned to God. I'm using it in a more general way here.

Testimony is the report we receive from a person who either heard it from someone else or used one of the other tools, such as perception, to get the information.

Suppose someone comes stomping into the house with delight and shouts, "It's snowing outside!" We use that testimony as a reason to believe it's really snowing. Of course, it entirely depends on whether the person giving the weather report is the kind of person who would tell the truth. If it's our mischievous older brother who loves teasing us, we may not have a good reason to believe it's true that it's snowing outside. But if these words come from our loving mother who has just pulled out our mittens and pointed us toward our sleds, then there's no reason to believe she's lying to us. We have a good reason to *know* that it's *true* that it's snowing outside.

Testimony, along with the other ways we know things, is a vital part of understanding history, including Christian history. When someone says Jesus rose from the dead, we want to ask, "How do you know?" And if they give the testimony of someone with good character who actually saw the evidence, then we have good *reason* to believe it's *true*.[29]

5. MEMORY

Looking back into your childhood, what's the first thing you remember? I remember sitting alone in a waiting room after my sister was born. I was about three years old at the time.

How do I know I was in that waiting room? I have no time machine to verify it with perception. But I do have my *memory*.

What is memory? You know this one. Autobiographers depend on this tool when they're writing books about their lives. *Memory* is our abil-

[29] This is exactly what we find in the New Testament, and we'll touch on this more in Question 4.

ity to recollect the past. Some people's memories are better than others. But if someone asks us about yesterday's weather report, we'd be telling the *truth* to say, for example, that it snowed three inches in the morning and the sun came out after lunch. How would we *know* that? Unless we suffered from amnesia or some other disorder, we can rely on our memory to give us the right information. This is yet another tool for knowing something is true.

Both memory and testimony are very important in a court of law. In a trial, witnesses are asked what they *remember* (memory) about a crime. And they're asked to *testify* (testimony) about it. If we cannot rely on memory for knowledge of the truth, then we could not depend on the witness in the courtroom. If we could not depend on the witness, then we'd never know if a crime was really committed. If we cannot *know* that, then criminals would never find justice, and we should all be very afraid.

A lot of our well-being depends on our ability to remember and make accurate testimonies. A healthy society depends upon, among other things, this tool of epistemology!

These are the five tools we use to know if something is *true*. Learn them. Memorize them. Understand the concepts behind them. They're vitally important in the Wild, as we're surrounded by people who've lost their ability to know truth.

With these tools you and truth will become friends.

By the way, these tools will continue to show up throughout this book, even if I don't specifically point them out to you. Be aware. They're necessary as we talk about the existence of God, the reliability of the Bible, the value of every human, and how to remedy our wrong desires and our loneliness in the Wild.

WE ALL WANT IT

The Matrix forces us to ask the question, "Do I want truth or ignorance?" As one character, Cipher, cuts into a juicy steak created by the Matrix, he says with a contented sigh, "Ignorance is bliss." But is Cipher correct?

WOULD WE WANT TO BE THIS GUY?

While I was working on my master's degree in philosophy, one of my professors told a story about Gunther.[30] Gunther was a foolish fellow. In high school he never knew the right answers, and he always raised his hand at the wrong times during class. It was so disruptive that instead of continuing to try to stop him, one teacher decided to play a joke on him. He secretly told the rest of the class to play along. Whenever Gunther made a comment, the teacher would congratulate Gunther on his insight, while the other students nodded and patted him on the back. Even if his answers for biology homework on the parts of the cell were all wrong, it didn't matter. Everyone praised him as a brilliant student.

Then Gunther graduated from high school and went to college. The high school teacher contacted the college and informed them of the big joke they'd played on Gunther. The college professors liked the idea and played along as well. Every paper Gunther wrote received high marks. He was voted "most popular" by his fraternity friends. And, to his delight, girls on campus flirted with him.

Finally, he graduated from college at the top of his class and went on to graduate school. Again, the joke continued, and Gunther excelled to the top of his class, even though he understood nothing of his coursework. Eventually, believing he was a genius, he pursued a doctorate, and he was chosen as *Time* magazine's Man of the Year because of his work in astrophysics.

Gunther believed that he excelled in his field. But the *truth* is that the whole world was playing a joke on him.

Here's a question for us to ponder: *Would we want to be Gunther?*

We all desire to receive high grades, popularity, romance, and even lots of money. But in Gunther's case, are these things worth it if they're based on a lie? A huge joke?

Gunther's story reveals something about truth and about all of us. It tells us that truth is a very valuable commodity—and we all want it. However, popularity, romance, and money don't have any real meaning when they're undeserved or divorced from the truth.

---

[30] This is a version of the story told by philosopher J.P. Moreland.

The Matrix taught us the same thing. The conversation between Morpheus and Neo about the real world and the computer-generated world applies where most people live today. Morpheus offers Neo a blue pill and a red pill. If he takes the blue pill, he'll go home, wake up, and believe whatever he wants. But if he takes the red pill, he'll see more of the *truth*, even if that road is a more difficult one to take. When Neo hesitates to make his choice, Morpheus adds, "Remember: All I'm offering is the *truth*, nothing more."

Neo swallows the red pill—not for popularity, success, or money, but solely to find out the truth.

For Neo, truth was worth the price of his life. And as a viewer of the movie, I wanted Neo to make the same decision. That's why the movie was a smashing success.

People want truth.

In the end, truth—not ignorance—is closer to bliss, even if it means new challenges. It's good and it's worth getting. Seeking the truth isn't always the most fun, but it's good because we have the assurance that we aren't living a lie.

Napoleon Dynamite captures this idea. Napoleon represents something in all of us. We want "skills," and deep down we're afraid that no one will love us if we aren't good at something. Napoleon learns at Rex Kwan Do that "you need someone to watch your back at all times." After that Napoleon meets Pedro, and they strike up a friendship. Throughout the rest of the movie, we see Napoleon use his drawing skills, speech-writing skills ("Tell them if they vote for you, all their wildest dreams will come *true*"), and his most-entertaining dancing skills to help his friend.

We know it's better to be a good friend than to be popular. We really want Napoleon and Pedro to defeat the snobby, yet popular, Summer Wheatley. Truth, including moral truth, is what makes life (and movies) meaningful, gives direction, and ultimately expands our *true* friendships.

In fact, even atheists appeal to truth when they tell religious people to give up religion. They say religious people are living a lie. So whether or not you believe in God, there is still this thing called *truth* that presses in on all of us. People want it. They appeal to it in an argument. And they expect others to see it, too.

RELATIVISM

What I've come to realize is that people are confused not only about truth but also about *relativism*.

Relativism—or skepticism—says we cannot know truth because we have no access to the real world. This view says the five tools of epistemology cannot work.

Most people don't live this way. They still pay attention to their gas tank gauges, they're still friendly at parties (because it's true that people will enjoy your company more if you're friendly), and professors still submit articles on skepticism because they're not skeptical that doing so will help their careers.

However, most people don't believe in this kind of relativisim that says nothing is true. Instead they define *relativism* as "viewing truth as *relative* to a particular situation." For example, "The sunshine is warm on a Caribbean beach"—is that statement always true? Not during hurricanes! And not when the sunbeams can't break through and kiss the sand.

Or take morals. The Ten Commandments say, "You shall not kill." But is that always the case? If you're protecting yourself or another innocent person from an evil person, killing the attacker may be the moral thing to do. If you're a government protecting your citizens from an enemy attack, killing may be the moral thing to do. Killing is *relative* to these situations, but it isn't *relativism*.

Relativism would say we'll never know. We'll never know if the sunshine is warm on a Caribbean beach—ever! We'll just never know if killing is right or wrong—ever! Relativism says we are free to invent what we believe about the sun or about killing because we'll never know what is true about those things.

Let me offer some clarity. You can believe in absolute truth and still believe that different situations require different ways to apply truth and morals.

Absolute truth only means there is such a thing as truth and justice. So we want to find it and apply it the best we can in a given situation.

Absolute truth says there is an *absolutely* real world and real situations to be discovered and understood.

I find that most people accept this explanation. And this view is also my view. Sometimes there are factors that change a situation, but we still appeal to our epistemology tools, and we still apply morals and justice, and we still appeal to truth to navigate what's true and false, right and wrong.

I've never actually met a real *relativist*. At some point, they're just regular people who believe in truth at some level. They still believe they have real cars that are parked in the lot. They believe they have real boyfriends or girlfriends, not just imaginary friends who call them on imaginary telephones. Plus, a real relativist has to admit they believe relativism is true. But that would be a contradiction because relativism says *nothing* can be known to be true—including relativism.

A HARDER LOOK AT FAITH

Doesn't Christianity tell us to have faith? Yes, it does. But we can no longer believe that faith means what many in our culture try to make it mean.

After my encounter with the police, I was in hot pursuit of answers. *What's the best way to live? What's my purpose? Why should we trust the preacher? Or our parents? Or the Bible?* But many adults just looked at me and said, "Have more faith."

When people in our culture talk about becoming a Christian, I've heard them repeatedly say it requires *faith* to believe this Christianity stuff. Or they say, "That's your faith, and I have mine," as if faith makes things true.

After giving a talk about truth in front of a thousand people, I watched a mother approach the aisle to ask a question at the microphone. Her posture was stiff and determined, as she clutched the silver microphone and blurted out, "How can I teach my children about truth when I'm trying to teach them to have faith?"

Those are tough moments. You know what needs to be said, but you must be sensitive to the parents who earnestly want the best for their kids.

So this is what I asked her, "If God answers your prayers, does that increase or decrease your faith?" She said it increased her faith. I went on to explain that an answer to prayer is evidence that God is listening. This tells us faith grows when we water it with truth. So faith and truth cannot work against each other. They're friends.

We've been told for too long that faith is the opposite of thinking and the opposite of truth. We've been told that in order to have faith, we must turn off our minds, stop looking for evidence, and give up on truth.

Faith has less to do with figuring out if something is true and more to do with trust as we enter relationships.

Many of the intelligent people I talk to who are skeptical of Jesus, often have a deeper obstacle to overcome. It's not that there isn't enough evidence to satisfy their minds; it's that they have a hard time trusting anyone, even God.

Jesus was concerned that we not confuse *faith* with *truth*. That's why he confidently says, "I am the *truth*" (John 14:6). He doesn't say, "I am the faith." He's saying truth points to him. He claims to be the ultimate starting point of truth. No amount of "faith"—in one way or the other—changes who Jesus is.

Faith in the Old Testament is always connected to a certain quality of faithfulness or trustworthiness. It has something to do with dependability. If someone is faithful, it means they can be counted on and trusted.

The best example of this is God. Repeatedly God is called "faithful."[31] He can be counted on to keep his promises. Yet we'd never say God uses faith the way many use it today. We'd never say God is thoughtless or makes blind leaps or is against the truth.

In the New Testament, the word *faith* is used in a similar way. The storm was thrashing out on the sea. Freaking out, the disciples went below deck to find Jesus sleeping through the storm. When they expressed their fears to him, Jesus said this to the disciples, "You of little faith, why are you so afraid?" Then he went on deck and told the wind and sea to be still (Matthew 8:25-27). Here, faith is contrasted with fear. *If you knew my character and that I'm in your boat,* he essentially told them, *then you'd know you can trust me to take care of matters. I'll make all things well.*

---

[31] Deuteronomy 7:9; 32:4; 2 Samuel 22:26; Psalm 33:4.

FAITH HAPPENS

Let's look at a chair. If you see one nearby you, analyze it with me. First, it makes good sense to say the chair exists. My eyesight (perception) shows me that it exists. My touching it (perception) shows me that it exists. It doesn't take any faith to know the chair exists. We actually have *knowledge* of the chair.

Now I must go on to the second step and examine the character of the chair. How is it constructed? Is it sturdy enough to hold a person? Has it held people in the past (memory)? We have *knowledge* of the character of the chair. None of this deduction requires an ignorant form of faith to study the existence and character of the chair.

So where does faith come in?

Faith happens when I enter into relationship with that chair. I'm not talking about asking the chair on a date. Rather, I'm talking about resting in the chair. Faith happens the moment *I rely on the evidence and actually trust* the chair to hold my weight. That's the moment of faith.

Another example is my wife, Jonalyn. Before we started dating, I had no problem believing Jonalyn existed (perception). And I remembered what a friendly person she was with other people (memory). People even told me Jonalyn is a friendly person (testimony). I gathered evidence that she has the kind of character that would make a good girlfriend. Where does faith come in? When *I rely on the evidence and actually trust* Jonalyn to return the friendship I offer her. And, to my delight, we started dating.

Notice carefully that faith is not the opposite of evidence or reason or truth. In fact, faith is what happens when I choose to follow the evidence to its proper conclusion. This fact is most important when we think about God.

The same statements I made about the chair and about Jonalyn can also be made about God. There are numerous reasons for believing God exists, as you'll see in the next chapter. And evidence about God's character is found in the Bible (testimony), in the world around me (perception, memory), and even in history (testimony). Throughout the Old Testament, we see how well God keeps his promises and expects others to do the same. When they don't, they suffer the consequences of their own actions. But when they do, God is committed to keeping his promises. And God cannot contradict himself (reason). So where does faith come in?

Remember, faith happens when I enter into relationship with God. It's when *I rely on the evidence and actually trust* that God will keep his promise to me. That's the moment of faith.

Faith has *nothing* to do with ignorance! In some places in the Bible, faith is called a "gift" from God (Ephesians 2:8, 9). And it's not a gift of stupidity.[31]

Faith has everything to do with trusting something when there is good evidence to believe it's true. Faith is having confidence in the character of something that has shown itself reliable. When we read the New Testament and replace the word *faith* with the word *trust*, it will offer us a better understanding—most of the time. Faith is not the opposite of reason and evidence. Faith is the opposite of pride, distrust, and fear.

At the beginning of this chapter, you wrote your definition of *truth*. Now I want you to write your new definition of *truth*.

What is *truth*? Define it.

If one day you're given a survey and asked to answer whether or not you believe in absolute truth, you'll now have a more confident response to give. You know the truth about *truth*.

LIVING OR DYING FOR TRUTH

On April 20, 1999, two student gunmen ran through the hallways of Columbine High School. Before their shooting spree ended, 13 people were dead. I've been to Columbine and walked the school grounds. I've stood beside the baseball field that's now dedicated to Dave Sanders, the only teacher who was slain that day.

[32] This line is borrowed from a former colleague of mine, Michael Ramsden.

During their rampage, Eric Harris and Dylan Klebold burst into the library. One of them put a gun to a student's head and asked, "Do you believe in God?"

The student replied, "No."

Then the gunman turned to the next student, Cassie Bernall, and asked, "Do you believe in God?"

She answered, "Yes."

"Why?" the boy replied and pulled the trigger.

Why? Because *true* religion is right for everyone. Why? Because it's better to die in the *truth* than to live a lie. Gunther taught us that lesson when the whole world played a joke on him.

Both Cassie and her killer died by gunfire that day. If you had to die as the gunman or Cassie, which would you choose?

QUESTIONS TO LIVE INTO

Grab a piece of paper and find a place to sit and write. Note the objects around you. Write down a list of three of those objects. Then write down three ideas or images that pop into you head. Then write down what you had for breakfast, lunch, and dinner yesterday. Then try to pair the items on your list with the different tools of knowledge. For example: I had cereal for breakfast. I know I had cereal because I used the tool of memory.

In your own words, explain what this statement means: *True religion is right for everyone. False religion is right for no one.*

If you could be Gunther, would you want to be? Why or why not?

Why is it that most people aren't real relativists?

Watch *The Matrix* with friends who have read this chapter. Discuss the theme of truth afterward.

Notes

_____

_____

_____

_____

_____

_____

_____

_____

_____

_____

_____

_____

_____

_____

_____

_____

_____

QUESTION 3

IS GOD THERE?

IS GOD RELIGIOUS?

I'm sure I looked silly sitting in my Jeep and shouting at my radio. But they were missing a huge point.

I was listening to a talk-show interview on a Los Angeles radio station. One person said "under God" should be removed from the Pledge of Allegiance because the First Amendment says "Congress shall make no law respecting an establishment of religion." Then he insisted, "God is a religious idea."

That had me shouting!

A "theist" is one who believes in a god(s) or goddess(es). And you don't have to be a "religious" person to be a theist.

God is not a religious idea, either; there are many reasons to believe God exists without relying on any religious beliefs at all. God's existence certainly doesn't depend on a holy book to tell us, nor does God's existence depend on organized religion. Just because many religions believe in a God doesn't make God a religious idea. Many religions say it's a good idea to feed the poor, but we don't believe that feeding the poor is a religious idea. We actually believe the government should help the poor. We don't want to cut welfare programs just because religious institutions and the government both agree it's good to help the poor. These ideas are good ones whether or not a particular religion or government believes them.

So let's be consistent. The ideas that God exists or that the poor should be fed are good or bad based on their own merits—and regardless of any religious or government approval. Our goal is to figure out what makes sense, not shun an idea simply because a person or a group we don't like happens to believe in it, too.

We cannot rule out the existence of God simply because some religions also say there is a God. We want to evaluate whether it's reasonable to believe God exists regardless of what any other religion believes. And if we determine that it's reasonable, then God wouldn't be just a religious idea.

If God exists, it's not because a religion made up God.

If God exists, then God is real—

• Whether or not someone believes in God

• Whether or not the government gives you freedom to worship

• Whether or not you want God in your life

"Does God exist?" or "Is God really there?" are questions as old as they are new. People thought hard about these questions well before Jesus came to earth, before Buddha explained Nirvana, and before Abraham was called a friend of God.

FEARING THE DARK

When I was young, I feared the dark.

I remember a special lamp shaped like a pelican that sat beside my bed. It was my companion on my journey to morning. The pelican watched the night while I slept—evening after evening, year after year.

When the house moaned and creaked in the night, I'd often stare wide-eyed at the ceiling and pull the covers close to my face. Sometimes I'd peek through the window above my bed, clicking the lamp off first so any prowler on the roof would be unable to see me. For half an hour, I'd stare out my window and wait for the house to hush, watching as a few random cars passed by on the street below my second-story window.

My fear often drove me into my mother's room in the middle of the night. I'd drag the comforter off my bed, tiptoe to her room, and settle into the carpet. It felt safe in her room with the crickets chirping peacefully outside her windows. I could fall asleep there.

My fear of the dark was really a fear of what could be *in* the dark.

When Karen babysat my sister and me, she'd tell us about the creepy man in the closet and how he'd come out and eat me during the night.

"What about my sister? Will he eat her?" I trembled.

"No. Only you," she leered.

When I was in my early teens, our house was burglarized while my sister and I were at school. At the time I felt even more vulnerable than I realized. We got a house alarm after that, something I'd begged my mother to do for a long time. The alarm system gave me a modicum of assurance that if someone dared approach our house, the cops were on their way. After that, the pelican lamp could sleep, too.

As I got older, there were more things to fear in the dark. But it was a different kind of darkness that haunted me. When I read the questions that students write to me now, I can see a similar darkness behind their questions.

Why did my sister die?

How come I'm always doing the wrong thing, even when I don't want to?

Why did God take my mother when I still needed her?

Why do people talk about peace but they don't know how to make it happen?

Darkness is—

• When we're afraid our parents are in debt and they won't be able to pay the rent—or help with our college tuition

• When a father yells at or belittles his daughter

• When a kid is burdened to obey "the rules" in order to be loved by his parents or others at church

• When someone has fears that nuclear war will destroy life as we know it

For me, my personal times of darkness happened when a friend betrayed me, leaders unjustly expelled me, my father left me, and the doctors discovered my mother had cancer.

Feeling hopeless in darkness and unawareness happens both *in our souls* and *out there in the world*. It leaves us teetering on the edge. It awakens our senses and threatens to paralyze us.

C.S. Lewis' *The Voyage of the Dawn Treader* paints a metaphor of how the darkness within us can haunt us from the outside, too.

Lucy, Edmund, and Eustace enter Narnia through a picture on the guestroom wall in England. Now on King Caspian's ship, the *Dawn Treader*, they join the quest to discover seven lost lords.

Voyaging from the Lone Islands to Goldwater Island to the Island of the Dufflepuds, they find several lords. As the captain turns the ship toward the unknown Eastern Seas, they see a dark cloud floating on the water.

They sail right into it.

The darkness is dense and threatens to snuff out their lamps. Then they hear a scream and sail alongside a man struggling in the water—it's one of the lost lords. They pull his frail body aboard. His wide eyes are sunken into a pale face, and he urges them to turn the ship around and fly, for this is the island where dreams come true.

At first, this news sounds awesome to the sailors. But the man screams, "Not daydreams, but NIGHTMARES!"

Everyone stands silent, just staring at each other.

Then panic!

The rowers run below deck and plow the waters at full strength. The ship turns in circles as dangerous noises grow nearer, sounds akin to grumblings and giant monsters from the darkest nightmares they've ever known. They row harder, shouting and gasping.

Lucy stands perched on the crow's nest at the top of the mast. She grips the rail and remembers her last hope—Aslan, the King above All High Kings, the great Lion who defeated death and the White Witch.

"Aslan, if ever you loved us, send us help now!" Lucy cries.

Lucy notices a tiny speck of light. In front of the light, an albatross draws nearer, circling the boat to lead them out of the darkness.

As it circles, it whispers to Lucy, "Courage, dear heart," and breathes a delicious smell on her face. She knows it is Aslan, and the albatross leads them as they punch through the darkness and back into the wide blue world again.[33]

---

[33] C.S. Lewis, *The Voyage of the Dawn Treader.*

When we face our dark places in the Wild and feel overcome by desperation, we have a great need for someone to rescue us when we need it most.

Is God there? If so, why can't we see him?

EMPIRICISM

I struggled hard over God's existence in my teenage years. That question alone troubled me.

Up to that point, I really thought I believed in God. But when I looked in the mirror and seriously asked my reflection, "Does God exist?" I hesitated to answer.

I was struck on perception as the only tool for knowledge. And since I couldn't smell, see, hear, taste, or touch God, I thought that maybe he wasn't real.

Some grown-ups at church would say, "God is like the wind. You cannot see the wind, but you can see its effects." But that didn't help me because the wind could still be *touched* (one of our senses of perception). I can *feel* the wind when it whisks away my breath on a high mountain peak or when the gales of a hurricane brush up against a beachside town. The wind was much easier to perceive than a God who could not be detected with *any* of my senses.

I often hear questions from students that are similar to the ones I had. Many teenagers assume empiricism (em-PEER-i-sizm) without giving one thought about it. And it's empiricism that causes us to raise these kinds of questions.

What is *empiricism*? Remember the five tools for knowledge?[34] An empiricist says perception is the **only** way we know things. Practical empiricists talk in terms of test tubes and telescopes and "science has confirmed..." and "I have to see it to believe it."

I was an empiricist, and I didn't know it.[35]

After I was arrested on that Halloween night, I went to a bookstore to look for something to help me answer my new questions. I thumbed

[34] See "Five Tools for Knowledge" in Question 2.

[35] Empiricism is used in philosophies such as naturalism and materialism. These philosophies say that only matter exists and, therefore, only our perception of matter is needed to find truth.

through a few books in the science section. Yet the topics that intrigued me the most were in the philosophy section. These authors dealt with the questions I was asking. Uncertain of which books to buy, two on the shelf caught my attention. One was *Pensées* by Blaise Pascal. It was a quotation book full of Pascal's ideas about religion. The book looked less intimidating because I could read the quotations one at a time.

The other book interested me because of an endorsement on the back. It said this author "is the ideal persuader for the half-convinced, for the good man who would like to be a Christian but finds his intellect getting in the way." Whether or not Christianity was what I wanted, here was a book that appealed to my curious mind. The book was *Mere Christianity* by C.S. Lewis.

I never considered myself a deep thinker. But I did have questions, and I wasn't hearing satisfying answers to my questions in the church my mother dragged me to every week.

Each night I read from these two books. "Faith certainly tells us what the senses do not, but not the contrary to what they see," wrote Pascal. "It is above, not against them."

"Faith" or "trusting the character of something or someone" was not *against* my senses but *above* them. Pascal was saying I should not expect to detect spiritual things with my sense of perception because the senses don't detect spiritual things any more than a thermometer can tell you that rape is wrong, or that Benjamin Franklin's kite can tell you the value of love.

I needed to use the proper tools to get at the question I was asking. And my spirit, not my senses, had the tools to detect spiritual things, tools such as introspection and reason.

Pascal spoke against the empiricism I assumed as a 17-year-old. I realized I was an empiricist and that empiricism was too limiting and closed-minded to help me with my question about God's existence. I needed a bigger philosophy—one that allowed for other tools of knowledge.

BEYOND IDEAS

A student wrote me, "I have a hard time believing God is even there even though I really want to. How do you know he is there?"

That's a question that bothers us from head to toe. Ideas matter and true ideas are the most important to seek out. But when you're in the dark, you want more than ideas. You want another person to help you out. You want the security and peace that a better, stronger, and smarter person is out there.

This chapter is about that Better, Stronger, and Smarter Person.

Fifty years ago the Communists tried to answer this question with empiricism and a spaceship.

In the late 1950s, Russia sent the first cosmonauts into space. When they came back, they announced something shocking. They claimed they were certain that God did not exist. Why? Because they looked for him in space and did not find him.[36]

What do you think of this announcement? Do you say, "See? I knew it!" Or "That makes sense, but I don't like it!" Or do you say, "I never expected God to be found in outer space!"

WHAT DO WE EXPECT GOD TO BE LIKE?

Let's think through this for a moment. How did the cosmonauts know God wasn't hiding from them? Perhaps God tricked them and hid behind the planet Mars until they went home. Or perhaps he was on vacation to another galaxy for the week.

NOT BOUND BY PLACE

Or consider what we might *expect* God to be like. People often talk about praying for those they love. They ask God to help them or be near them when they're in battle, facing cancer, or suffering abuse. All these assumptions mean we believe God can help us, even if it means doing so in more than one place at a time.

In the movie *Forrest Gump,* an abusive father chases his little girl, Jenny, through a cornfield. Once she's beyond his reach, Jenny drops to

[36] Some say this is folklore—that it never happened this way. Regardless, we still live in the scientific age that says if we can't detect God with our senses, God must not exist. Even if the cosmonauts didn't say it, many people (professors, students, scientists, politicians, etc.) believe and act similarly today.

her knees and says, "Dear God, make me a bird so I can fly far, far away from here!"

These prayerful expectations of God mean that we *expect* God is not a physical being.

Physical beings can only be in one place at a time.

How can God be available to hear all of your prayers or be near you if God cannot be in more than one place at time? If God were merely physical, then he wouldn't have that ability any more than the president can be with everybody all the time. If we expect God to be near and to hear our prayers, then we don't expect God to be limited by the physical universe. We don't expect God to have a body. We don't expect God to be made of stuff that can be perceived with our senses. We expect God to be *spiritual.*

NOT BOUND BY TIME

We'd also expect God to hear all prayers at all times and be able to answer them in some way. Consider the movie *Bruce Almighty*.

When Bruce temporarily takes over God's job, he's bombarded by so many prayer requests that he has no time to look at each one. So out of frustration he answers *YES* to all of them! The next day people riot in the streets because too many people won the lottery, and each winner received a payout of only $17.

We know God must be bigger and better than Bruce.

If we pray to a God who exists, then we expect God not only to have the ability to hear all prayers at once but also to be the kind of being that has enough time to think about and answer them all. We expect, then, that God is free from the limits of time. We expect God to be *spiritual.*

GOD IS SPIRITUAL

Where does that leave the Russian cosmonauts? If God is spiritual, then we'd never expect him to have a body or be visible to our senses. No voyage into the deepest regions of space can tell us anything about whether or not God exists. It would be like using a GPS to find your purpose in life. Science is the wrong tool or instrument to find God.

GOD IS STRONG AND SMART

Even beyond God's ability to answer prayers and be near to us, we also expect God to be very smart and very strong.

If God designed the universe, then he must be the most intelligent and thoughtful Architect. The universe is extremely complex with its gasses, quarks, distances, genomes, biomechanical organisms, the beauty of sunsets, and a midwinter fire flickering in a hearth. If God exists, we'd expect him to be big enough to make the world, our solar system, our galaxy, and the whole universe—all 15 billion light years across! We'd also expect God to be wise enough to orchestrate every law of physics and understand the breadth of human need on our tiny blue planet.

That's very, very smart.

If God created the universe, God also has to be strong.

We hire earth-moving equipment to erect new buildings. Yet God had no construction team to put this universe together. We expect him to be extremely powerful in order to not only put it there, but also to keep it there and keep it functioning in a well-ordered splendor of light, space, gas, and motion.

WHAT ABOUT THE SIZE OF THE UNIVERSE?

An "atheist" is someone who is not a theist—or, more precisely, someone who claims God does not exist. I've heard atheists say we shouldn't consider ourselves too important to God because he made us so small and surrounded us with a universe so big.

That idea should give us pause. It's *possible* that our smallness is an indication of our unimportance. After all, if prayers worked like radio waves, it would take billions of years for our prayers to reach the edge of the universe.

Yet, if the universe is intended to be our dwelling place and if God can hear prayers while they're still on our lips, then the size of the universe produces for me the opposite effect.

Consider this: If a wealthy parent built a bigger house for his kids to enjoy, then would we say he doesn't care for his kids? Does a cold, uncaring parent design pools with waves and slides, adventure parks, tree houses, go-karts, closets full of clothes, and a bunch of other cool stuff?

Maybe God, like a wealthy parent, made the universe big in order to show his care for us more extravagantly. But the size of our planet and the surrounding universe has nothing to do with God's existence. That makes about as much sense as someone believing that the larger the basketball, the more important the game.

The brilliance of God is that he made us exactly as he intended. Granted, the size of our planet can tell us many things, but one thing it doesn't tell us is the value of a thing or a person.

So if God exists, these are things we expect God to be: Spiritual, Smart, and Strong. And if we expect these things from God, then we have to find evidence beyond empiricism (perception). Let's look in another direction.

IS JUSTICE REAL?

Jonalyn tells a story about a group of guys who cut in front of her in a line at Disneyland. When she neared the front of the line, the attendant asked her, "Did those guys cut in front of you back there?" Yeah, they were cutters, she admitted. So the attendant told those guys they had to go back to the end of the one-hour line. The attendant grinned at her and said, "This is the best part of my day." Justice served.

At 17, I was looking for evidence of God's existence. In *Mere Christianity* C.S. Lewis points out something so obvious that I didn't even think of looking there. It had to do with people cutting in line, quarreling over candy, hurting each other, and desiring to make things right. He says our expectation for justice points outside ourselves.

I understand fairness and quarreling. If someone cuts in front of you in the lunch line, for example, you want to protest. And if you do, the cutter may give you reasons to justify why he cut. And then you might show him why those reasons are still wrong. But he may just say, "Too bad! I'm not moving!" One thing that's worse than injustice is when people don't care that they've hurt you.

Indeed, justice isn't always served:

People take our saved seats at the movie theater.

People are stingy even after we've shared our stuff with them first.

People tell us we can borrow things and then change their minds for no good reason.

People are nice to our faces but trash us behind our backs.

Classmates borrow our homework and copy it as their own.

Parents divorce, are abusive (physically, emotionally, or verbally), and drive us to dull the pain of life with drugs, cutting, casual sex, and melancholy isolation.

When I started to collect baseball cards, I bought several packs and took them to my friend's house. He already had a collection, and I wanted his advice. When he saw my new cards, he traded with me. A few days later, another friend of mine told me about pricing guides, and I soon realized I'd been duped by one of my best friends. I was so angry that I broke into his house one afternoon and "traded" all the cards back.

Later, I felt guilty. So I confessed what I'd done and gave the cards back. *Fairness, quarreling, justice, injustice*—the issues pressed on me from every side. But in the end, we must realize that justice is important and accessible to everyone.

Imagine this scenario:

An attractive guy reads his magazine over a latte in a local coffee shop. There's a less attractive girl sitting across the café from him. He looks at her.

She lifts her eyes to meet his, and then quickly glances at something else, trying to pretend she didn't notice him watching her.

He closes his magazine and moves to her table. Now he looks deeply into her eyes.

She's starting to blush. Nothing like this has ever happened to her.

"Pardon me," he says, "I find you very attractive." He reaches out to hold her hand in his.

She tries to catch her breath. This is a moment she's always longed for, but she thought it would never happen to her. Finally, she manages to speak in excited half-breaths, "Really?"

"No, I was only kidding." As he slips out of his chair to leave, he mutters under his breath, "You're too ugly for me to look at."

Once outside, his friends laugh and hand him five bucks.

I want someone to kick that imaginary coffee-guy in the teeth! Is this scenario unjust? Does it point to something really wrong? We sense deep within us that what this guy did is not only unpleasant, but it's also *mean.* There's something twisted about that guy, and we want him to get what he deserves.

What would an empiricist say? Remember, an empiricist relies on the tool of perception alone for truth. So when it comes to morality, an empiricist can only speak about his emotions. Something isn't good or evil—it's only pleasant or unpleasant.[37]

When the unattractive girl leaves the coffee shop in tears, all an empiricist can say (if he's consistent) is, "It isn't *wrong* of that boy to do that to you. It's just unpleasant! Good and bad are only how you *feel* about it, not what things actually are."

That's a tough argument because our feelings are usually involved in these kinds of situations.

The empiricist is correct that it's unpleasant. It hurts. Yet not all hurts are evil. Sometimes hurts are good—like when a drunk driver is hurt by having his driver's license revoked.

But unpleasant feelings are often a thermometer for something deeper going on—a gauge on our dashboard that tells us something is awry under the hood.

[37] This empirical view of ethics is called "emotivism" and was championed by the prince of empiricism, David Hume.

The guy in the coffee shop didn't insult *me*. He said nothing about me. My feelings were not hurt. Yet something has gone wrong.

THE ORIGIN OF JUSTICE

But where did we get this idea of justice and injustice? Is it just a feeling? Or is it something real in the world?

Martin Luther King was a champion for civil rights. He believed that African Americans were just as human as European Americans (those with lighter skin). Racism ran deep in America, and King spoke against it in the '50s and '60s. Was he just sharing his feelings on the subject?

Let's suppose for a moment that he was. If so, his speeches would've sounded something like this:

Ladies and Gentleman: I don't feel good when I see black people sitting in the back of the bus or when black people cannot get jobs because of their skin color. I'm not saying it's wrong or anything, I'm just stating my feelings. And my feelings are more important than anyone else's feelings. And I think everyone should share my feelings because I want people to do what I want.

Compare that with what King actually said:

*Now is the time to rise from the dark and desolate valley of segregation to the sunlit path of racial **justice**. Now is the time to lift our nation from the quicksands of racial **injustice** to the solid rock of brotherhood. Now is the time to make **justice** a reality for all of God's children...*

*I have a dream that my four little children will one day live in a nation where they will not be **judged** by the color of their skin but by the content of their **character**.*[38]

So was King simply sharing his feelings, or was he talking about real rights and wrongs that were understandable to everyone? If we say it was just his feelings, then we disgrace King's sacrifice and make racism a per-

[38] Martin Luther King, "I Have a Dream," August 28, 1963 at the Lincoln Memorial, Washington, D.C.

sonal preference—in other words, "choose racism if you prefer racism." We'd never be allowed to call racism vile, wrong, evil, bad, or unjust.

But if we say racism is a real problem, then justice and injustice must exist as real factors in the world. King believed we should be judged not by our skin color, but by our character—living by what's right and wrong.[39]

If justice and injustice are only feelings, as the empiricist insists, we shouldn't say that mean people are actually mean. We can only say we don't *like* their behavior, or it isn't *useful*. But if justice and injustice are more than feelings—if they're something *real*—then it's only sensible to call mean people "mean." And it's sensible to take a stand against social injustice, such as taking care of the poor, speaking out against child abuse, reporting people who starve their pets, or supporting judges who put murderers in prison.

Injustice cannot be a matter of feelings.

JUSTICE WITHIN

If justice and injustice are real factors, then how did we get these ideas? When I was reading Lewis's opening chapters in *Mere Christianity* (which I recommend you read—they're short, so go for it!), I was struck with a new awareness.

I looked inside my own soul (introspection). While I could observe everything else in the universe from the outside, there was something I could observe from the inside: ME. I could see justice and injustice within me as well.

This concept didn't come from society, for people (such as King or Jesus) often sought justice against society and even changed society. Today, every headline in the newspaper talks about corruption in economics, world politics, international sanctions, and pollution.

People desire justice with an intensity that comes from a standard inside of them. With that standard they want to make things right for themselves and for others.

---

[39] This is a big statement by King. He isn't saying we shouldn't judge; he's saying we should judge according to justice and morality. Many people today forget how appropriate this is.

This sense of justice pressed upon me from the *inside*. Something deep down jumped up whenever I saw injustice happen. It's the thing that made me feel troubled when my friend and I thumbed through the pornographic magazines. It was the thing that shocked me when I was arrested and I realized I was on the wrong side. It was the thing that wanted someone to kick the guy who insulted the girl in the coffee shop.

Justice and injustice (or "right and wrong") were closer to me than anything I had thought about before. It was closer than all the objects in the world that I could detect with my senses. Those objects were always on the *outside*, but my measuring stick of right and wrong was on the *inside*.

It was even closer to me than my own family and my friends. It was so close that it went with me everywhere I went, whether I liked it or not. I could try to drown it with music, television, or activities, but it kept showing up as soon as the silence came. It was part of me.

But where on earth did it come from?

Using our reason again, let's think about it:

• If there really is a sense of justice within us, then this means a justice-giver actually placed it there.

• Maybe *we* gave it to ourselves. We could claim we *invented* it. But that would be like saying we invented mathematics. Sure, sometimes we need instructors to guide us and teach us algebra and calculus, but that doesn't mean our instructors invented mathematics.

• But if justice was invented, why would we expect others to have invented the same standard of justice? Why would we force our ideas of justice on others (which is what we do any time we tell someone that racism is wrong or they shouldn't betray their friends or they shouldn't pollute the atmosphere)? Are we supposed to advertise all the morals we invent to make sure everyone else is forced to adhere to them?

• Okay, we *discovered* it. Once upon a time we didn't know the Pythagorean Theorem, but it still existed. Justice is the same way. We understand it better the more we follow it. But it's *discovered*, not invented. For example, we *discovered*, not invented, that cheating hurts others, corrupts society, and even makes us feel guilty. And when we see people cheating, we usually don't immediately think of society or how that person won't succeed in the future. We usually think, "That's so wrong! That punk!"

• We *expect* people not to take our seats in the movie theater. We *expect* people not to talk badly about us when we're not around. We *expect* men to treat women with dignity and as their equals. We *expect* it because we *expect* other people have discovered justice within themselves, too.

• It presses on everyone! Even if they run from it, drown it out, or ignore it. If there is a moral law, then where did it come from?

DOES SCIENCE GIVE IT TO US? I cannot find morals under a microscope.

DOES SOCIETY TEACH US? King went against society's teachings, as did Gandhi and Jesus. Plus, we believe they were *right* to disagree with society, and many people praise them as moral heroes.

DO OUR INSTINCTS GIVE IT TO US? Sometimes I have two instincts, and I have to choose the right one. I may have one desire to fight for peace and another desire not to be violent. The two compete against each other, and there's a proper time for each response. It's justice that shows me what to do and when to do it.

DID OUR FAMILIES GIVE IT TO US? I admit that I did learn a lot about morality from my family. But when I think about it, I find I disagree with my parents about some moral issues and expect them to change as the *right* thing becomes clear. And my concern about violating the laws of right and wrong is much deeper than any concern I may have about crossing my family. The law of justice actually got stronger as I grew older.

When I was 10, I was riding in the car with an adult relative I respected. He asked, "Why do women get so upset when you sleep with other women?" He was just thinking out loud. He probably felt guilty about something. But the question flew out of nowhere, and I felt embarrassed. The thought had never crossed my mind.

I blurted out, "Well, it's just not good!" Even though no authority figure had ever taught me that sleeping around is wrong, I just knew it was.

My family didn't give me the law of right and wrong. It's just there, like a hunger for love is just there.

The law of right and wrong is deeper and larger than science, society, instincts, or my family. That narrows my search down to just one option that makes sense to me.

The best explanation I have found is that the spiritual, smart, strong being is also the Justice-Giver. We call this being God—and God has built a moral law within us.

That would explain why everyone else—in every culture—has this sense of justice, too. No culture believes it's okay, for instance, for a neighbor to bully, terrorize, and kill all of their friends. And we call cultures that believe otherwise twisted and wrong (sometimes we even use words such as *primitive* or *savage*). And we praise international organizations that rescue kids abused in sex trafficking and stolen for war.

God, through justice, gives us a strong sense of how things *ought* to be.

There may be exceptions, just like there are people with color-deficient eyesight. (I'm color deficient, and I struggle to see shades of red and green.) But the general rule is that among healthy people in the entire human race, this awareness of justice is present. Some may disagree about the details, but it's difficult to deny that the law of right and wrong exists to help people figure out those details.[40]

MORALITY FROM CHOICE

If the universe just popped into existence, it would be difficult to explain justice. We'd simply behave according to instinct. That's it. And if instinct is all we have, then it's just survival of the fittest.

That's something to ponder. Many of the actions we perform are survival-based. We go to school so we can get a job to survive. We tell the truth to our teachers and employers to survive (because if they find out

---

[40] If you're looking for some examples, see C.S. Lewis' appendix in *The Abolition of Man*. He traces and compares the history of different cultures and their laws. There's a remarkable similarity among them.

we're lying, we may fail classes or lose our jobs). We resist cheating to survive (because we want to have real knowledge so we can succeed).

But can we think of some moral choices that people make that *don't* help them survive? The events of September 11, 2001, are a good example. Firemen and policemen tried to help people as the World Trade Center towers collapsed. Many lost their lives while helping others. We call those kinds of acts "heroic." Why? Because they can climb many flights of stairs? No—anybody can do that. Was it because they were good at driving fire trucks through New York City? No—I'm sure many taxi drivers could do the same.

They're heroes because they chose to resist their survival instincts in order to accomplish justice. They lost their lives for others, even if those others weren't necessarily popular or particularly smart.

Or consider parents who choose to give birth to their children, even though their children appear to have Down syndrome. Their lives would be much easier if they aborted the babies, as some doctors might suggest. Yet they keep the babies, not so they'll survive better and not so their new babies will have many children, but simply because they believe there is value in human life, regardless of defects and limitations.

This is heroic because it goes against the very instincts we'd have if we came about by atheistic evolutionary development. [41]

The truth is, we have a responsibility. We may have many instinctual impulses in our blood, but we're still responsible for what we do with them. We may be lost in the Wild, but we're not without a map.

THE FUTURE OF JUSTICE

If God did make the universe and intended for us to enjoy it in relationships, then we'd expect to find ourselves designed with a sense of justice within us. God wants us to choose to be in relationships and bring justice and peace into the world.

[41] I need to make a comment here about evolution. Notice that I use "atheistic" evolution. There is also such a thing as "theistic" evolution that does believe in justice. But theistic evolutionists also believe God created the world through the evolutionary model. You can believe in God, even the Christian God, and believe evolution is a fact. If you don't understand how, I suggest reading Francis Collins' *The Language of God*.

This would also explain why we feel guilty when we do the wrong thing and why we have a deep-down desire that everything will be right in the end—that justice will ultimately be served.

KARMA

This is different from the Buddhist idea of karma that's popular today. Karma, for example, says we get what we deserve. Yet, there are injustices done to people who weren't deserving of them. Child abuse is one such example. Some who believe in karma say a child suffers abuse because of something she did in a previous life; therefore, the child-abuser inst't unjust because he was only giving the child what she truly deserved.

However, justice is not about repayment. It's about making things right. It isn't a cycle that oscillates back and forth. Justice says that when a line goes crooked, we should try to straighten it again.

STORY ENDINGS

This desire for everything to come out right in the end is what makes many great stories work. Take *The Lord of the Rings*, for example. We want the Orcs to lose. We mourn the death of Rohan and the slaughter of free peoples. And no matter how bloody it gets, we celebrate with deep relief when the One Ring is destroyed and Sauron is no more.

To deny such a thing as justice is to say that Middle-Earth was not under the threat of the shadow. It's only to say a shadow is coming, and we're sad. It's neither good nor bad in itself. Either Sauron or Aragorn could be the ruler—it makes no difference. There is no moral hero because there is no morality.

Because we long for everything to be just and right in the end, we love the story. It taps into something deep within us that philosophy books have a hard time describing. Stories are not only enjoyable, but they reveal how our souls long for justice every day.

It's because of justice that I believe God exists.

A RESPONSE TO ATHEISM

In his book, *The Rebel,* atheistic philosopher Albert Camus writes, "For twenty centuries the sum total of evil has not diminished in the world." He doesn't try to explain it away with instinct or psychology or anything like that. Camus saw that evil was everywhere and that the human race was swimming in it.

The usual atheistic response is that if God exists, then he wouldn't allow all the injustice we see. God would step in and stop it.

It's hard to argue against this viewpoint, especially when you've suffered and have seen people you love suffer. We want God to do something, too! And our desires aren't new. The writers of the Psalms cry out over and over again, asking God to do something with injustice.

But for Christians, the Triune God is the only one who's ever dealt with the problem of injustice by taking it upon himself in Jesus Christ's death and resurrection. The atheist simply leaves us without any god, stuck in the mire of injustice without a way out of the Wild.

Yet, notice that this argument does not dismiss God's existence. Rather, the atheist risks *validating* God's existence. How?

As I've already noted, if God doesn't exist, then justice doesn't exist, either. Without God we have no ultimate standard maker—we have no straight to measure the crooked. *Crooked* only makes sense when it's compared to *straight.*

The atheist demands that the Straight fix all the crooked and then determines that since there still are crooked things, clearly the Straight cannot exist. Yet, how does the atheist know what *crooked* is without first knowing the meaning of *straight*?

When the atheist says God cannot exist because God isn't as just as she'd like him to be, she's using justice to say the Giver of justice is unjust. Is she admitting that everyone else knows about this mysterious justice? My question to the atheist is, "Where did you get that idea of justice, and why do you expect everyone else to understand it?"

At the very most, the atheist who uses this argument can only say that God is unjust or inconsistent—not that God doesn't exist.

John Locke, whom many atheists celebrate as the forerunner to the modern world, made an often overlooked statement about atheism and how it stands in the way of justice. He said:

> [T]hose are not at all to be tolerated who deny the being of a God. Promises, covenants, and oaths, which are the bonds of human society, can have no hold upon an atheist. The taking away of God, though but even in thought, dissolves all.[42]

We can see that if God is not allowed into promises, covenants, and oaths—if God is not permitted to be an explanation for justice—then Martin Luther King and the rest of us would have no reason to suppress evil in our world. Who decides what is evil or good? It becomes a fight for power without any ultimate standard.

I was an empiricist atheist, until I studied this argument about justice. But I was stuck, and I had to get honest with myself. Before I could call God unjust, first I had to look at why I was unjust.

CONCLUSION ON JUSTICE

This sense of right and wrong presses on us all from the inside out, and God's fingerprints are there. After all, if we find justice valuable, then God must find it even *more* valuable since he gave it to us.

After I read *Mere Christianity*, I digested it and mulled it over. Then I set it aside for a while because it answered my question about God's existence with its argument about justice.

It convinced me.

But it wasn't only because of those reasons that I believed God existed. I could also feel the moral law deep down inside of me, and I couldn't run away from it. I started noticing it everywhere, too: its invisible presence in the morning news (the journalist thought this rape was wrong), across

[42] John Locke, "A Letter Concerning Toleration," 1689, translated by William Popple, (http://www.constitution.org/jl/tolerati.htm)

the Internet (should Britney Spears be allowed to raise her children?), and in my daily conversations and choices (was it really my responsibility not to pirate music?).

C.S. Lewis helped me notice something inside of me that had always been there. Something I'd never thought to consider—not only is God near, but he also knows about my darker secrets.

If I had broken God's law, then I wondered what God thought about me.

It's one thing to wonder if God is there. It's another to know if God is there on friendly terms.

BECAUSE WHY?

It isn't merely justice that points in the direction of God's existence. More clues make me believe God exists. And the more clues I have, the more convinced I become.

Science may not have the authority to talk about these clues because the clues aren't detectable with perception. Scientific facts can only tell us how things *are*, for that's all perception can describe. It cannot tell us how things *ought to be* because how things *ought to be* is beyond our perception.

Think of it like this:

You gather with some friends at a construction site on the edge of town. A friend walks up with a pipe in his hand. It's plastic and curved at a 45-degree angle. He's twirling it. You look at the pipe.

Suppose I drive up just then, and I lean out the window and ask, "What's that pipe supposed to be made of?"

Weird question, right? Let me try again.

"What's the shape of that pipe, and what's it made of?" I ask.

"It's a bent, plastic pipe."

Exactly! Now back to my first question, "What's the pipe supposed to be?"

That question is still unanswerable without knowing more information. And that's the point.

It's impossible to explain how the pipe *ought* to be or is *supposed* to be without knowing the larger picture. Perhaps that pipe is supposed to join together a water line. If that water line needs to bend at a 45-degree angle, then that piece of pipe is a perfect fit. However, if the water line needs to remain straight, then that pipe is worthless. But we don't know what the pipe *should* be, until we know what it's for.

In other words, *What's the purpose of the pipe?*

These words—*ought, should,* and *supposed to be*—haunted me as a student. Like justice, they're built into us. We wake up one day and start asking the question, *Why?*

Why is the kettle on the stove?

Why does she clean her jewelry?

Why are we here?

What is the purpose of school?

What is the best way to live?

Why am I asking why?

Why is built into us. I wouldn't expect this to be the case if we'd popped into existence by the random chance of an atheistic Big Bang. How do I know that?

Well, if the universe came about by accident, and if we're just a bunch of DNA strands and atoms thrown together, then I don't expect us to ask "why?" Atoms just bounce around according to the laws of physics.[43] Asking "why?" would be unnatural. Rocks never ask "why?" Neither do clouds or birds or my dogs. Humans are the only ones who ask "why?"

---

[43] These "laws of physics" are also unexplainable in a random universe. All laws have law-givers. What people often call "laws of physics" are just repeated incidents they see happening. For example, gravity predictably happens all the time. So it's called the "law of gravity." But again, laws have law-givers. Who made gravity act the way gravity acts? Who caused it to perfectly balance the universe? Those who believe the universe is based on random chance have no answer for this. It isn't a "law." It just is. That explanation bothers me because it feels like something important is being ignored.

If we're just randomly bouncing atoms, then we'd just take things as they are—the same way a computer does.

The atheist Richard Dawkins agrees when he writes in his book, *River Out of Eden*, "DNA neither knows nor cares. DNA just is, and we dance to its music."

"Why is she cleaning her jewelry?" would never be asked. She'd be cleaning her jewelry just because she's cleaning her jewelry. There'd be no reason for it. Randomly bouncing atoms don't have reasons. They just bounce. DNA just is. It doesn't dance with a purpose.

We'd be as clueless as that bent pipe if there were no larger purpose for us on the earth. We'd simply take the world as it is and live in the Wild without uttering a single question. But our questions remain. And the questions themselves are a clue to God's existence and a clue to get us out of the Wild.

There's something mysterious about us, as if we're a caged bird with a nagging sense that we're far from Home. We're more than dancing DNA.

Think about this question with me for a moment:

Why is the grass green?

I once asked a group of students this question, and one of them shouted, "Chlorophyll!"

"That tells me *how* grass is green," I replied. "It doesn't tell me *why* it's green and not some other color." At that point, everyone sat still.

We only have two answers to choose from: 1) It just is, or 2) Someone wanted it to be that way.

If we choose the first answer, then we have to wonder why I was born into a "just is" universe while *reason* tells me to ask why something is more than "just is." It's like I don't fit in.

"Just is" doesn't satisfy my question. It doesn't even *validate* my question. It silences me the same way you'd silence an outspoken, annoying kid. It tells me I'm weird for even having a question. But then every human would be weird. So maybe atheistic evolution isn't a reasonable explanation.

On the other hand, if we choose the second answer, then suddenly the universe opens up many possibilities and many larger purposes.

This is a form of the **teleological argument**. *Teleological* comes from the word ***telos.*** This ancient word means "end." Or to put it in our terms, "What is the end of a thing? Or the purpose of a thing? Or the real point of a thing?"

When I asked, "What's the shape of that pipe?" I was asking a *descriptive* question.

When I asked, "What shape is the pipe *supposed* to be?" I was asking a *teleological* question. I want to know its designated purpose.

And guess what? Science cannot answer teleological questions. Teleological questions are outside the discipline of science. Science can only describe what a thing *is*. It cannot tell us **why** anything exists. If we go to science to answer questions about our purpose, we're going to the wrong place.

Who made us ask this question? Is it a clue that God wants us to live into an answer?

In her book, *The Spiritual Life*, Evelyn Underhill writes, "The meaning of our life is bound up with the meaning of the Universe." If objects in the universe—such as grass, kettles, staplers, hair gel, and pipes—have meaning, then how much more is there a purpose intended for something as multifaceted, complex, and curious as you and me?

(Notice I'm not talking about answering the "why" questions. Many answers are still mysteries. I'm just pointing out our natural desire to raise the "why" questions. The human mind and experience speaks loudly and clearly that we're looking for the "why" of things.)

It's the ongoing need to ask *why* that puzzles me.

If God doesn't exist, I don't see why I'm asking *why*. This haunted me.

C.S. Lewis remarks in *Mere Christianity* that,

Creatures are not born with desires unless satisfaction for those desires exists. A baby feels hunger: well, there is such a thing as food. A duckling wants to swim: well, there is such a thing as water. Men [and women] feel sexual desire: well, there is such a thing as sex. If I find in myself a desire which no experience in this world can satisfy, the most probable explanation is that I was made for another world.

There is, of course, no guarantee that we will be satisfied. But at least this is an indication that Something is there that might be able to satisfy it, if we can find it.

It's a hint that God is encouraging us to ask *why* because, I suspect, "why" will eventually lead us to God.

George Herbert says as much in his poem, "The Pulley," which is a picture of how our desire for another world pulls us back to God, who made us. Herbert speaks of God allowing us to be restless, removing from us the jewel of complete rest. Here's part of it:

> *For if I should (said he)*
> *Bestow this jewel also on my creature,*
> *He would adore my gifts instead of me,*
> *And rest in Nature, not the God of Nature:*
> *So both should losers be.*
>
> *Yet let him keep the rest,*
> *But keep them with repining restlessness:*
> *Let him be rich and weary, that at least,*
> *If goodness lead him not, yet weariness*
> *May toss him to my breast.*

We'll find that our biggest questions lie beyond the Wild and the little closed world of empiricism.

And we may better understand why God allows us to be restless with questions.

Because our restlessness drives us to find the God of Rest.

WHERE DID IT ALL COME FROM?

There's one more reason why I want you to consider God's existence. It's called the **Cosmological Argument.**

Cosmological comes from *cosmos*, which means "the whole arrangement of the universe working together." So in talking about the beginning of the "cosmos," we're talking about the beginning of the universe working together.

This argument is as basic as potatoes and requires little explanation. The version I like simply says this:

> *All things that have a beginning have a cause.*
>
> *The universe had a beginning.*
>
> *Therefore, the universe had a cause.*

That's pretty easy. So did the universe have a beginning? Absolutely. That's what Big Bang Theory is all about. It's largely agreed, even in the scientific community, that the universe had a beginning.

Looking at it simply, if the universe had a beginning, then it had to have a cause outside of itself in order to begin. What caused the universe to come into being? Our options are pretty limited.

It had to be something that wasn't made of matter, or else it wouldn't be outside of the universe. Therefore, it must be something spiritual.

To make something like the universe and something as complex as the human mind (that seeks justice and asks *why*), this spiritual being would have to be pretty powerful—smart enough to orchestrate it and strong enough to *choose* to orchestrate it.

So for me, the most reasonable explanation for how the universe began is a spiritual, smart, and strong being. Aristotle called God the "First Cause."

On the heels of that explanation, it's not unusual for students to ask, "But who made God?" I love that question. But that question doesn't fit here.

We're only looking at things that have a beginning. We know the universe had a beginning. And now that we know, it becomes *unreasonable* to say God *cannot* exist. God fits right in. "Who made God?" is a different question. For now, we at least know the universe had a beginning. And therefore it's reasonable to conclude that God exists.

THE RELIGIONS OF THE WORLD

Perhaps you're thinking, *Okay, if God exists, how do you know which religion is right?*

That question comes up a lot. And it often carries the assumption that no religion is allowed to claim it's the right one. But that question is still beyond the point I'm making here.

For right now, I'm just trying to show that it's reasonable for us to conclude that God exists.

If God doesn't exist, then nothing really matters but the random bouncing of atoms, or our diversions, or society's vote, or the purposes we have to invent for ourselves. We could just silence and stuff our questions, though we'd be stuck with some poor reasons for why we have a sense of justice, why we ask *why*, or how the universe got started. But in my own journey through the Wild, God's existence makes the most sense.[44]

If God exists, then we have a few more questions we need to answer before we can assign God to a particular religion. (Remember, God is not a "religious idea.") So if we're in search of the right religion—if there is such a thing—we want to start with what God is like and then find the religion that best describes God.

But what kind of God is he? Is there anything that gives us a clue?

Well, based on this chapter, what can we conclude about God? I'll let you list some characteristics here before I go on (sometimes the answers are more obvious than you realize). What do *you* think God would be like?

_____   _____

_____   _____

[44] See "Intermission—A Few Special Rules" after this chapter.

Now that you've listed some, let me share some of mine.

• *I find God good.* If God cares about justice and wants me to care about justice, God is good and wants others to be good, too.

• *I find God smart and strong.* Not only did God put the universe together, but he also put "purpose" into it as well. That we naturally ask the "why" question means God likely has answers to our questions, not that God will tell us all of them. But we can at least be assured that as we live with our questions for God, we have a good chance of living into the answers.

• *God is a person.* What do I mean? I mean a couple of things. *First, God cares.* God cares about the kind of environment we live in. In this environment, God also put a lot of other humans who have a deep desire to love and be loved. God cares that I'm a being who cares about relationships. God cares that I belong. Caring is something only persons do. Therefore, God is a person. *Second, God created the world with intention.* Non-persons don't have intentions. I've never seen a rock decide when to turn over. I've only seen persons decide to do things.[45]

So, if God exists and created the world with morality and purpose, then God has personality. God is a person with a free will, for God freely chose the universe to be created in a way that could nurture all kinds of life.

These are just simple things that we can gather from the arguments for God's existence. I believe most people—if they put aside their religious views or family history or their gripes against God—can see these characteristics of God as well.

Well, here's something to keep in mind. And I don't mean to put anyone down. I just want you to think about this idea.

Some religions of the world say "God" is *not* a person.

Does that make sense with the way we find the world to be? Why care about goodness, intention, purpose, and meaning if there is no reason why or how those things could even exist?

[45] When I say "God is a person," I don't mean "God is human." Persons have personality, and there can be many things with personality that are not human. Take science fiction, for example. Beings from other planets are persons, even when they aren't human. Or look at the land of Narnia. In that world there are talking beasts. They are persons, but they aren't human. In our world there really are only three different kinds of persons that we know of—humans, angels, and God. (You may choose to include demons, but demons are just angels gone bad.)

It seems to me that if God is impersonal, then we are back at a pur-poseless universe with some all-powerful but non-personal force behind it all. We're back to random chance putting things together. Only instead of physical randomness, it becomes spiritual randomness.

I have a friend in India who says many people there think much like the atheists here. Instead of believing that the *impersonal material* world is all there is, they believe the *impersonal spiritual* world is all there is. Either way, the problem is the same. We're boxed in with nobody, no person, no one to answer our questions, on the outside.

That just won't work if justice and purpose are real things to be fol-lowed. So, to me, it doesn't make sense to explore religions that don't explain the world as we find it. We need to find a religion that does.

Unfortunately, this rules out some of the major world religions, such as Hinduism and Buddhism, as many forms of Hinduism, Buddhism, and other Eastern religions are **pantheistic.**

PANTHEISM

What is **pantheism**? (*pan* = "all"; *theism* = "belief God exists") It's the view that everything in existence *is* God. That's much different than say-ing God *made* everything. Instead, God is the rock, the tree, the bird, the dog, you, and me.

Some pantheists claim that if you have spiritual experiences in na-ture, then you may be a pantheist. This isn't true. People from all differ-ent points of view can have spiritual experiences in nature. You're only a pantheist if you believe God *is* nature and if, in some way, you're part of God yourself.

If everyone is God, then God is good *and* evil because humans are both good and evil. Justice disappears because God would be fighting against himself. And there doesn't seem to be any hope in the end. Why would you worship or trust God if God is also evil?

If everyone is God, then when we contradict each other—who is right?

Much of the history of pantheism in India is a sophisticated form of superstition religion from more than 2,000 years ago. And if you visit there, as I have, that impression is very strong.

A couple years ago I visited the city of Varanasi. Among the many impressions I had, one in particular really moved me.

We climbed aboard a rowboat on the mighty Ganges River. As we paddled away from shore, I looked back to see thousands of people along the shoreline and on the steps leading into the water. Some were drinking from the river, some were bathing, some were using it as a bathroom, some were brushing their teeth, and some were scrubbing their clothes.

I could also hear bells ringing, hundreds of them. They were calling people to worship. The incense filled the air as people shuffled around cows to come to the river.

A few hundred feet farther down, fires burned. This was the crematorium. If you could afford it, your body would be burned beside the river after you died. Then the remains that would not burn would be thrown into the river.

The Hindu man in our boat said the Ganges is the holy river. He said the waters are so pure that if you bottled it, it would be cleaner than any bottle of Evian drinking water. As he said this, a floating candle drifted by the boat and some human remains. The river ran thick with mud.

I wondered why he would live in such contradiction to the evidence. Anyone could see the water was not pure. My perception and reason confirmed it.

That is superstitious pantheism at work in Hinduism. We were told the river is holy, and every creature is to return to the river's spiritual source. Their belief system says it's holy, and that makes it holy.

I normally would have been skeptical that this represented true Hinduism—I usually don't find people whose beliefs are so contrary to the evidence. But it is. In fact, Varanasi is the spiritual center of Hinduism in the world.

HOROSCOPES

I believe the desire for horoscopes, which is a growing trend among American students, fits in with this as well.

If the universe is mindless, many people are going to search for comfort in whatever superstition they can, even if it doesn't make sense.

Some believe those born on the same day in the same hospital have the same disposition toward sensitivity or defensiveness. Or they look to the stars to guide them in their everyday choices.

Yet, what tools of knowledge confirm that certain people are born with the same predispositions? What tools tell us the stars hold our futures? If there is no personal God, then why should we believe the stars are trustworthy guides? And if there is a personal God, why would the stars be more trustworthy than God?

BUDDHISM

In similar fashion, Buddhism says God is just a mysterious impersonal force all around everything and in everything. If you've seen the *Star Wars* films, you'll understand where George Lucas got his ideas.

But if the universe requires a good, smart, and strong being who has a will to cause it, then an impersonal force just doesn't explain things in a satisfying way. We may call it *positive energy*, but that doesn't get away from the difficulty. It's still *impersonal*. That's the problem.

So based on the reasons I've described in this chapter, I believe there really are only three general religions that believe God is a person: Judaism, Christianity, and Islam.

IS LOVE POSSIBLE?

Now let me throw one more clue out there. If God is personal and cares about us, then God is a loving Creator.

Love is an interesting thing because it cannot exist by itself. I've never seen love floating like a feather on the wind. It must be inside a person and acted out by a person. Nothing impersonal, whether physical or spiritual, can exercise love.

But even that's not enough. I cannot love if no one else exists. There would be no one to love. Love requires another.

I've heard people reply, "Well, that's why God created the earth and humans—so he'd have someone to love." This was the answer I got in church. At first it made sense to me, but then I really started to think about it.

DOES GOD "NEED"?

Unlike humans, God is God. And God is self-sufficient. He doesn't *need* anything. It would be weird to say my Jeep is self-sufficient as I put gas into the tank. It isn't self-sufficient. It requires energy from something else.

So if God *needs* humans in order to show love, then God isn't self-sufficient. God would *need* something else to love.

But if God isn't self-sufficient, then he isn't God. He's just a bigger version of us (like the Mormon god). And if the whole world refuses to love God in return, then we can actually make God needier!

So God must be both loving and self-sufficient, even if the whole world chooses to ignore him. What must God be like in that he can be both...and still be God?

More than one person is required. There would need to be at least two—or maybe three—within God himself. This would allow God to love for all eternity because he could love other persons in himself. Each of these persons would need to be uncreated and existing from all eternity. Each would need to be loving in God and self-sufficient in God.

The strange thing is, of all the religions that believe God is loving, only one says God is loving *and* self-sufficient from all eternity. That religion says God is a Trinity. And that religion is called Christianity.[46]

(Did you notice that I didn't need to open any Holy Books or quote any passages from the Quran or the Bible? These aren't "religious" ideas, they're ideas we can reach by taking time to think hard on the way the world is.)

PRAYING AND HOPING

Let's return to the beginning. We find ourselves in the dark, and we're afraid of what's in there. We want someone who is bigger, smarter, and stronger than the danger that lurks.

---

[46] Christianity says (as stated in Deuteronomy 6:4), "Hear, O Israel: The Lord our God, the Lord is one." This means God is self-sufficient. No other god(s) exist. Christianity also tells us in Philippians 2:6: "[Jesus], being in very nature God, did not consider equality with God something to be used to his own advantage." The Holy Spirit is also part of the Godhead. Jesus speaks of the "Spirit of truth" in John 14:15-18. Here we see three persons, but we know from Deuteronomy 6:4 that they are one. When Jesus was baptized, all three persons were present (Matthew 3:16). To formulate these ideas in a simpler way, Christianity teaches that God is three persons in one essence. God is both self-sufficient and loving at the same time, from all eternity.

At the same time, we're born into the Wild, which is also full of danger. Our parents may be able to protect us in some ways when we're little. *But what happens if tragedy takes them? What happens if they die? Can they protect us from that loss? What happens when we feel rejection from others at school? What happens when we feel guilty about our own bad choices? What happens when we're in this kind of darkness? Is there hope?*

While I was speaking to a group of students, one gentle girl in the group, a Buddhist, spoke up as we talked about prayer. She was trying to argue for prayer from a Buddhist perspective.

"Prayer," she said, "is the hope I have for someone to be well or for a good outcome."

"So prayer is hope?" I asked.

"Yes, it is hope," she replied.

A couple of dozen students (and Jonalyn) were sitting around me, and they listened to my response. I shared the story of Hurricane Katrina and the havoc it wreaked on New Orleans. Half the city was flattened. Scores of people died. News coverage revealed the terrible devastation to the world.

Many said, "We *hoped* the buses would be ready! We *hoped* the levees would hold the water! We *hoped* people would evacuate!"

Many critics responded, including CNN reporter Anderson Cooper, "Hope is not a *plan!*"[47]

I stopped my story and explained how hope is not enough unless it's grounded in someone who can do something with our hopes.

The room was silent for a few moments as agnostics, atheists, and this young Buddhist considered the problem. If God does not exist, then who can offer us the plan to get out of the Wild that we all hope for? How can we reasonably consider that our prayers are heard?

When it comes to the darkness I find in the world, I want more than feelings of hope. Plans bring real hope, but hope is not the same as a plan. An *impersonal* physical or spiritual force cannot offer a plan. Nor do randomly dancing atoms offer a plan. Only a person can offer a plan.

Like Lucy perched atop the *Dawn Treader*, I need Aslan to fly in and lead the way out.

---

[47] Anderson Cooper, *Dispatches from the Edge.*

I find that only God is good enough, loving enough, smart enough, and powerful enough to find me and help me through the dark.

QUESTIONS TO LIVE INTO

Take some time to note what you're thankful for. Write a list. Then see how each of those things can come from God and his good character.

Have you ever experienced the law of justice inside of you? When?

How does the law of justice point us to God's existence?

Go online and Google words from this chapter such as *empiricism, pantheism, atheism,* and *Buddhism.* Read what the articles say. Make notes about what appeals to you and what doesn't make sense. Are some of the things that appeal to you also found in the Christian God? Write in the margin why some of what you read just isn't reasonable to believe.

Ask some people at school if they believe God exists—and then ask why or why not. Do they seem willing to talk about it? Have they even thought about it much? See what kind of discussion happens.

Notes

LIVING WITH QUESTIONS

INTERMISSION

A FEW SPECIAL RULES

Let's take a break from the heavy stuff for a moment. What are we supposed to do with this information? After all, does this *prove* God exists?

Let me lay down some rules.

RULE #1: IT'S DIFFICULT TO PROVE *ANYTHING*

To prove something means that it's impossible to doubt it.

You may be able to show me that you can tie your shoes, but you can't prove it. You may even show me lots of evidence that you can tie your shoes. You could even demonstrate it to me in front of 500 people. Yet that still doesn't prove it. Why? Because I could be dreaming. I've dreamed things like this before. Or perhaps *you're* dreaming. Perhaps you only *think* you're showing me you can tie your shoes.

Someone can always play the "Prove It" game. But I don't play that game. It's unhelpful. Countless people have said to me, "Oh yeah? PROVE IT!" It's a game people play when they want to be right, and they want you to shut up. (It's not a very nice game either.)

So what do we do?

RULE # 2: WE AIM TO BE REASONABLE

If someone plays the "Prove It" game with you, tell them you aren't trying to prove anything. If they're still listening, you can continue…

You're trying to show that what you're sharing is *reasonable* or that it makes good sense.

What's more, you're trying to show them, as well as yourself, that it's more *reasonable* than believing the opposite conclusion. For example, it's more reasonable to say the stoplight is red than to say it's blue.

Instead of shooting for 100 percent proof, consider shooting for *75 percent*. That's all you really need. There will always be some reasons not to believe something. But that doesn't mean it's *unreasonable* to believe it.

RULE #3: THE MORE REASONS THE BETTER

My wife and I enjoy watching episodes of *Columbo* on DVD. This detective uses his powers of observation to collect all the evidence and pull the case together. He'll interrogate the suspect with his seemingly irrelevant questions, "You know, I can't figure out how that scuff got on the wall." And the suspect creates some sort of explanation. But that explanation will have to fit all the other evidence about the body being carried from the driveway. And it turns out it's the wrong explanation. The right explanation will fit with the rest of the story and all the *cumulative* evidence.

It's important to look at the *cumulative* evidence on a crime scene. Even more important is looking at the cumulative evidence for God's existence.

What is *cumulative* evidence? It's all the evidence together making a big picture. You *accumulate* all the different puzzle pieces to form the whole puzzle. And if a piece just doesn't fit, then it does us no good to try to beat it into place.

I cannot prove God exists with 100 percent certainty. But the evidence that God does exist is more than the evidence that he does not. Too many puzzle pieces point to him. If I just believed God exists because of the argument from justice, then I may be on shaky ground if someone can show me that DNA does somehow care about justice. Yet, it still doesn't answer the teleological argument or the cosmological argument or many others. It doesn't disprove God exists. It just makes the argument from justice weaker. It loosens a piece from the puzzle that we thought fit there. But it doesn't loosen *all* the pieces of the puzzle.

Even still, it would be *unreasonable* for me to be an atheist. It's more *reasonable* for me to be a theist because of the cumulative evidence. And as you've seen in the last chapter, it seems even more reasonable for me to be a *Christian* theist.

These rules help us avoid playing the "Prove It" game and put us on solid ground. They also help us have some humility and go easier on people who disagree. If they don't think the point you're making is more *reasonable*, then let it be. There's no benefit in beating them over the head with it. (The "Beat People Over the Head" game is even worse than the "Prove It" game.)

All of life is like this. You can't prove to someone else that abortion is wrong or that a woman's choice is right. All you can do is appeal to justice and give arguments that are more reasonable in one direction or another.

Tying your shoes is the same way. It's more reasonable for me to believe you can tie your shoes than to believe you can't tie your shoes. After all, showing it to me in front of so many witnesses is pretty good evidence. In fact, it would be stupid of me not to believe you can tie your shoes, even though you couldn't prove it 100 percent.

RULE # 4: ASK FOR SOURCES

If someone persists their view is the right one, ask them for some books or articles to read so you can see their point of view better.

You can do this with teachers and professors, too. If you believe they're bullying the class to believe one way or another about God, ask them for more information. Jonalyn tells a story where a teacher was beating up Christianity in her college classroom. She raised her hand and asked, "Can you give me three or four scholarly articles that support your position?" The teacher fumbled. He didn't have sources. He was taking advantage of his academic position over his class of undergraduates. And he respected Jonalyn the rest of the semester.

If your teacher does give you some articles, then you have material to read to understand the position better and see whether it makes sense.

Now there's one caveat to this rule. If you ask others for their sources, you'd better have some, too. That's a good reason to read and watch and listen better. One day, someone may be depending on you for it.

QUESTION 4

HAS GOD SPOKEN?

While I was in college, I found a dock that hung out over a bay. I spent many evening hours there, away from everything—just sitting, thinking, and wrestling with my thoughts about dating relationships, project deadlines, friends, and the ways of college. While I couldn't solve these issues just by being there, I wanted to find some peace and know that Someone may be watching, speaking, and comforting me.

I often sat and listened.

A fish jumped.

The waves moved softly over the still water and onto the shore.

The bay mirrored the tiny specks of light in the black, velvety sky.

Unheard music flowed from the celestial bodies above, moving in their patterns and throwing their beams to earth like an extended, friendly hand. They moved to numbers, just as a piece of music does, and played their song. The ancients called this unheard music, "the harmony of the spheres."

Dangling my feet over the dock, I was comforted by the sea air, the star song, and the calm bay. I was not alone, but I was part of something bigger than my own questions. I was just a creature on a planet teeming with countless other creatures, where everything had its place and worked in harmony. The earth is filled with peace and fury, lights and fire, delicate sea foam and surging waves.

I remembered the words of the Psalmist:

The heavens declare the glory of God;

the skies proclaim the work of his hands.

Day after day they pour forth speech;

night after night they display knowledge.

They have no speech, they use no words;

no sound is heard from them.

Yet their voice goes out into all the earth,

their words to the ends of the world.[48]

[48] Psalm 19:1-4.

Creation blanketed me and provided enrichment for my body and soul. Yet creation is also created. Nature and I have this in common: We are both mortal. Nature is my friend and the habitat of my home—built by a God who loves.

God loves.[49] Love is in God's very being in the Trinity. If all the celestial stars and galaxies were collected into a universal fireball, God's love would still burn hotter, brighter, and wider.

God creates. He created the physical and spiritual worlds: the singing stars; the gentle, giant pelicans that soar in the vast sky and plunge into the deep sea; and the angels we rarely, if ever, see but sometimes hear about.

If this is God—Lover and Creator—then I would hardly expect God to remain silent. God must have something in mind for all the human creatures on our planet who cry out with their questions from lonely docks.

We experience something profound when we sit in nature. Something spiritual happens. Poets write about it, and the pagans reach out to worship it. William Wordsworth wrote about the mystery of nature in his famous poem, "The World Is Too Much with Us." By it, he means we've grown too familiar with nature's power and its mystery and its voice that goes out to the ends of the world. We've silenced it with technology, we've taken it for granted, and, sadly, it no longer moves us.

He writes:

The world is too much with us; late and soon,

Getting and spending, we lay waste our powers;

Little we see in Nature that is ours;

We have given our hearts away, a sordid boon!

This Sea that bares her bosom to the moon,

The winds that will be howling at all hours,

And are up-gathered now like sleeping flowers,

For this, for everything, we are out of tune;

[49] See chapter 3 about God's existence and relational qualities.

It moves us not.—Great God! I'd rather be

A Pagan suckled in a creed outworn;

So might I, standing on this pleasant lea,

Have glimpses that would make me less forlorn;

Have sight of Proteus rising from the sea;

Or hear old Triton blow his wreathed horn.

Wordsworth believes the pagans—even with their gods such as Proteus and Triton—have remembered something the modern world has forgotten. And this is something we would do well to pay attention to.

Nature is a signpost in the Wild, a clue to a more concrete hope that God has spoken to us of the way Home.

"How do I know God has spoken to me?" is a question students frequently ask. Sometimes they want to know what God's will is for their lives. Other times they want to know if God cares enough to speak. And if God *has* spoken—where?

GOD SPEAKS

When talking about God speaking, we must clarify what *speaking* means.

Sometimes we speak *verbally*. We talk to people in the classroom. Or we call them on the phone to plan the weekend.

Sometimes we speak with *writing*. We send thank-you notes to someone who invited us to the party. We text-message our friends when we're bored. We may even scribble in our journals or pen a poem.

Sometimes we speak with our *actions*. We give a wink or a knowing look to encourage someone across the room. We help friends wash their cars. Or we visit the sick in the hospital.

Communication happens in many different ways. And we must give God the courtesy to choose the modes he knows are best.

It's unfriendly to demand that a friend call us only at a certain time of the day. And it's obnoxious to visit a sick person at the hospital after visiting hours have ended. (If you've ever been sick in the hospital, you know what I mean.)

If God created us, *he knows the best ways for us to hear and understand what he wants us to hear and understand.*

God does not play hard to get, although it sometimes *feels* that way. That's not the way God's kind of love works. God has deliberate reasons for speaking the way he does.

Bertrand Russell, the famous atheist, was once asked, "When you stand before God, what will you tell him?"

He replied, "Not enough evidence, God, not enough evidence!"

Yet I believe people sometimes demand loud evidence when God may be offering it softly. Or they demand that God write them a personal letter when he's already written letters for all of humanity. What we demand from God before we really get to know him will usually determine the kind of evidence we require from him. We want God on our own terms.

We see the same struggles in our everyday relationships. We require that someone show us their affection by sending us flowers and cards. Or we require they give us more physical attention. Or we require they spend so much time with us each day. Eventually our demands look less like friendship, or even a boyfriend-girlfriend relationship, and more like owner and pet.

If God is as good, loving, and smart as he appears, then he won't give into these kinds of demands. Nor will God usually give us reasons for showing us his love in certain ways—ways that sometimes bypass our defenses and come as a surprise.

Isn't it true that receiving flowers without making any demands for them feels all the sweeter? And aren't dates all the better when there's mutual desire rather than feelings of obligation?

As one journalist said, "God speaks not in whirring of sirens or the grinding of brakes, not in the policeman's whistle or the newsboy's shouting, nor computers driving the information superhighway. But in a still, small voice. If only one could catch it."[50]

Many people believe that if God really exists, he would start talking to us and spilling out evidences that are undeniable. I mean, why doesn't

---

[50] Adapted from Malcolm Muggeridge in *Chronicles of Wasted Time: The Green Stick.*

God just peel back the sky and shout, "I exist! Look at me! Here I am, look at me, Rebekah, Jose, Samantha, Kio, Ted, and Lin!"?

But what would that look like? God is the uncreated First Cause of the Whole Show. God is the One who holds love and radiance in his very Person. God is the Fountain of life, light, and pure goodness. God resides in the land of Endless Day.

Once God started talking through the clouds or whispering to us through our closet doors, we'd freak out!

How do I know? Because we get freaked out when lesser beings do this to us. If a man puts a gun to your head through the open car window, the wise person would step out of the car, hand over the keys, and spare his own life.

Yet guns are puny when compared to God's power. And thieves are small when compared to God's presence.

We give in to peer pressure all the time just because we want to fit in. How much greater would the pressure be if someone as big as God were to come near us without disguise? Let's not fool ourselves about how we'd respond in such a situation.

And let's not demand that God speak to us in ways we cannot handle.

Or to look at it another way, suppose someone claims to have seen an angel or claims God spoke to him. What is our first inclination or knee-jerk response? Doubt. We more readily expect these kinds of tales from patients in mental hospitals.

So on one hand, we are too frail and too easily coerced by lesser powers than God. On the other hand, we usually disbelieve people who tell us that God or angels talk to them. If and when God gives us loud evidence, it isn't enough for most of us to freely choose him with an open soul.

That's not to say God cannot and will not speak in these ways. It's just that God knows us too well. If God is going to communicate to us, then God will choose a way that dignifies our will to choose him without feeling as though we have no choice in the matter. While we live in the Wild, God will choose a way that is *near enough* to affirm our minds and hearts, but at the same time still *far enough* not to overwhelm us.

Remember the end of first chapter: "There is a battle between Heaven and Hell over whether God is good. And the battle is for the human heart." This battle is not over swords but over love. God will not overwhelm us. God wants us to see that he is good and to follow in his love—freely. This is the battle of the universe.

So if God is speaking to us in gentle but affirming ways, he has done so as an Author sharing his life and love, and without getting in our faces about it.

And what happens when we don't notice the various ways God has spoken? We can grow arrogant to think that if we know the Bible, we know all there is to know about God. Or we become less confident if we believe the nebulous messages of nature are enough without learning about God's more particular revelations in his Word.

What has God authored? When we left the previous chapter, I concluded that since Christianity is the only religion that demonstrates God is relational in his very being as a Trinity, it only makes sense to explore what the Christian God has spoken.

Just as we communicate through various means, such as a letter or a knowing look, God shares his love with us in a variety of ways, including experiences with nature, written words, and himself.

OUR EXPERIENCES WITH NATURE

Jesus is speaking to a small crowd on a Galilean hillside. He says, "See the lilies of the fields and look at the birds."[51] He encourages his audience to see past weeds and wings. Who feeds these feathered friends? Who clothes these astonishing flowers? What is the meaning of this?

When we ask the question, "Has God Spoken?" we must look at the various ways God speaks. In nature God has created beauty and majesty and great power. Nature evokes something within us to pay closer attention to what it all means.

---

[51] Matthew 6:25-34.

INTO THE WOODS

While I was growing up, I spent a lot of time in the woods. I loved walking stealthily under the canopy of pine trees. And every Thanksgiving, I tested my skills when my dad and I went hunting together.

Our normal ritual was to set up a stand in a tree, and then we'd sit in it—absolutely still—for hours. We'd wake up early each morning, around 4:30 a.m., eat a bowl of cold cereal, and follow the reflective markers that lined the trail to our stand in the forest. We'd sit in that tree for at least five hours, just waiting for animals to cross the path. Then we'd break for lunch, only to repeat the same ritual in the afternoon until it became too dark to see.

As I got older, I'd go alone to my tree stand. The dark felt thicker when I walked there by myself. The forest floor pitched up and down. The vegetation grew thick and thin. Even the air warmed and cooled depending on where you stood.

Going to a tree in the middle of the woods—alone and in the dark—is frightening. When you suddenly walk into a warm patch of air, your imagination works on you. I'd start to imagine Bigfoot was breathing on my neck. So I'd stop and shine the flashlight behind me. Bigfoot disappeared. I continued walking to my next marker, more quickly this time, until I finally got to my tree. Then I tied a rope to my rifle, climbed the tree stand, and pulled my rifle up after me. I never worked so quickly in my life as when climbing a tree to escape my imaginary Bigfoot.

We have a good idea that Bigfoot does not exist. However, the forest is alive. Trees sway and grow. Critters with teeth and spines and fur and hooves all inhabit those places where I walked in the dark. I was part of something bigger than me. I was invading someone else's natural community.

In all those years, I never tagged a deer. Yet I learned to be still. Sitting motionless for five hours in the woods allows you to see things.

A raccoon passed by and quietly climbed a tree.

Squirrels played tag, dangling from limb to limb.

An armadillo swaggered through the swamp.

A fawn stepped into the open, followed by five doe watching, nosing the breeze, and bending their ears.

My heart bounded at the sight of those deer. These creatures tended the forest garden. They were velvety-brown rulers of the wood.

I didn't really have a firm belief in God when I was 11. Yet when a group of deer passed close enough for me to hear them chewing acorns, my response was, "Amazing, God! *Amazing!*" It was a spiritual experience. Time froze at a rare and meaningful moment.

INTO SPACE

On Christmas Eve 1968, *Apollo 8*, the first manned mission to the moon, did a live television broadcast from lunar orbit. After circling the backside of the moon, they emerged on the other side to see what no one had ever seen before—the Earth, a blue marble swirled with cotton clouds, coming up over the horizon. They were the first to witness an Earthrise.

Overtaken with the sight, the astronauts beamed back to Earth their Christmas message and finished with a reading from Genesis 1, "In the beginning, God created the heavens and the earth." After reading the first few verses, they said, "And from the crew of Apollo 8, we close with good night, good luck, a Merry Christmas, and God bless all of you—all of you on the good Earth."[52]

Of course, some may protest and say this kind of experience could evoke a reading from any holy book, not just the Bible. And they'd be right.

But what this reveals is that as humans, we sometimes have an experience with nature that points to something *beyond* nature and to its Maker.

NATURE RELIGIONS

Some religions actually focus on nature alone to hear the Divine. Again, this points to the fact that God can use nature itself as a means of telling us something.[53]

Wicca (Neopaganism) is likely the most popular nature religion in the West today. According to their own definition, "Wicca is a modern Pagan religion with spiritual roots in the earliest expressions of reverence for nature."[54] It believes that the Divine is in everything, and that by paying at-

[52] You can see and hear the actual transmission at NASA's Apollo 8 home page: http://nssdc.gsfc.nasa.gov/planetary/lunar/apollo8info.html

[53] I discuss pantheism in chapter 3. It's the worship of nature.

tention to nature and its cycles, Wiccans will grow more in tune with the Divine that's present in nature and in themselves (and in everyone else).

If God spoke to us only through nature and did not speak directly through his written Word, then I would be very tempted to join the Wiccan religion. In some ways, it makes sense. We do perceive something in nature. That's why the ancients peopled their rivers and mountains with gods. (Ever wonder where we got the names of our planets, such as Mercury, Jupiter, and Saturn?) The ancient Romans enjoyed the pleasures of Bacchus, the god of wine. In a world full of suffering and hardship, they expected and looked for a god to help them escape their troubles by offering them wine. Even King David wrote that God made "wine that gladdens human hearts."[55] The point is that they all saw something wonderful in nature's provisions.

Wicca is growing partly because people notice that more is going on in nature than mere atoms and chlorophyll—something meaningful that's overlooked by the tools of science.

Yet when I'm looking at nature, I wonder if there's a larger picture—something outside of nature that informs nature, something that is super-nature or supernatural. Part of that larger picture is the man called Jesus who came to earth and gave us some good evidence that he died and rose from the dead. If his death and resurrection is true, then it helps us understand more about what nature is supposed mean.

Jesus tells us to consider the birds and the flowers, how they eat and how they are clothed. Jesus never denies the power, beauty, and experience of nature. If anything, he makes it more meaningful. He shows us there is something behind the scenes *unifying* nature, making it all work together, a Person who cultivates it for our pleasure and our home.

Jesus says,

So do not worry, saying, 'What shall we eat?' or 'What shall we drink?' or 'What shall we wear?' For the pagans run after all these things, and your heavenly Father knows that you need them. But seek first his kingdom and his righteousness, and all these things will be given to you as well. (Matthew 6:31-33)

---

[54] This definition comes from www.wicca.com. It's important to use a group's own definitions, rather than simply putting a group in a box its members might protest. In fact, that's a good rule to use for anyone who believes differently than we do.

[55] Psalm 104:14, 15.

Nature is to be loved and enjoyed, but not worshiped. Worshiping nature, as stunning as nature is, would be like thanking my house for its nice cabinets and large windows.

I believe the atheist and the neo-pagan are in the same dilemma: Have they no one to thank? I remember reading G.K. Chesterton's remarks that if his children have someone to thank for putting gifts in their stockings on Christmas morning, do you and I have no one to thank for putting the gift of feet into our socks?[56]

BEYOND NATURE

One struggle I have with the Wiccan view of nature is not that it's too free, but that it's too limiting. It doesn't take into account that God may be speaking to us in other ways as well.

When I was searching for God, nature served as a signpost for me to keep looking for him. The poetry of the late Rich Mullins, a real lover of nature, helped me when he sang things like this:

There is such a thing as Glory

And there are hints of it everywhere

And the hints are overwhelming

And its scent is in the air

It's more powerful than morning

Oh, the morning can't compare…[57]

Or

From the place where morning gathers

You can look sometimes forever

Till you see what Time may never know…[58]

---

[58] "Calling Out Your Name," *The World as Best as I Remember It, Vol. 1.*

[56] G.K. Chesterton, *Orthodoxy.*

[57] "Such a Thing as Glory," *Winds of Heaven, Stuff of Earth.*

Or

Nobody tells you when you get born here
How much you'll come to love it
And how you'll never belong here
So I'll call you my country
And I'll be lonely for my home
And I wish that I could take you there with me.[59]

Or

Be praised for all your tenderness
By these works of your hands
Suns that rise and rains that fall to bless
And bring to life your land
Look down upon this winter wheat
And be glad that You have made
Blue for the sky and the color green
That fills these fields with praise.[60]

Rich Mullins was of Irish heritage, the same region of the world that developed the Wicca religion. He knew something about the meaning of nature and prompted me to pay more attention to it.

In his masterpiece essay "The Weight of Glory," C.S. Lewis speaks of the power of nature in sunsets, rivers, mountains, music, and imagination in books. He says these things

> in which we thought the beauty was located will betray us if we trust to them; it was not *in* them, it only came *through* them, and what came through them was longing…These things…are good images of

[59] "Land of My Sojourn," *A Liturgy, A Legacy, and a Ragamuffin Band.*
[60] "The Color Green," *A Liturgy, A Legacy, and a Ragamuffin Band.*

what we really desire; but if they are mistaken for the thing itself they turn into dumb idols, breaking the hearts of their worshippers. For they are not the thing itself; they are only the scent of a flower we have not found, the echo of a tune we have not heard, news from a country we have never yet visited.

Rich Mullins and C.S. Lewis helped me understand something about God. In the music of Mullins, I saw something special about nature. But I also saw *through* nature and glimpsed the greater meaning of it on the other side.

This view was such a contrast to what I found at church. Perhaps you've felt this way, too. When I entered the doors of my church, I saw a lot of superficially happy people, smiling and shaking my hand like greeters at Disneyland, just glad they got me through the doors.

Then the music we sang—considered "contemporary" for the "younger generation"—was dull and hardly imaginative, even though it was loud. Songs spoke about God and how much I loved him (which I didn't) and how much he had done for me in dry, religious-sounding clichés.

It all seemed unreal and detatched to me. There wasn't any meaning in it, or at least not the larger meaning I longed for that I'd tasted through the writings of the Christian authors and songwriters. Church didn't speak to my deeper longings.

Yet, all this while, I had no problem believing in the God of the prairies, the woods, and the sea. When I pondered the crashing ocean waves, I sensed God was there—not physically *in* the wave, but showing me something about himself *through* the wave. God was as real as the ocean, though I knew he wasn't the ocean. God was as real as the canopy of pines I sat under while I watched the deer, even though God wasn't in those pine trees. God's presence came *through* the sunrise. Those things were real. And my longings for the God of those real places drove me to find him and be near him.

One part of my journey was coming to realize that regardless of the people and programs at Sunday morning services, the God of the prairies was also the God of the church.

OTHER PEOPLE

In my late teenage years, I heard an elderly man talking about our planet. I remember he said something like this:

Somewhere in the galaxy there was a race of aliens who heard a rumor that on a tiny blue planet on the other side of space, there was a race of creatures who were made like God. ("Made in God's image" was the term they used.) The aliens thought if they could find this planet, they could find out what God is like.

This alien culture pooled all their funds and workers together to build a rocket to travel to the blue planet. Several were appointed for the mission, and they waved from the cockpit as the engines blasted them into space.

For months they flew to find the blue planet. And back home, the people eagerly awaited their return. They wanted to know what God is like.

Finally, the aliens landed their rocket on the blue planet called Earth. They threw open the doors and got their first glimpse. Then their hearts sank.

They saw human beings, made in God's image, exploiting each other. They stole, killed, swindled from one another. They said hurtful things, made rude comments, and were selfish. They created machines that polluted and raped the land. They competed with one another because of fear and power.

Departing, the aliens blasted their spacecraft toward home.

When they landed, millions of alien people circled the landing pad. Banners were held high. Shouts and cheers erupted. They were going to find out what God is like!

Then the rocket doors opened, and the crowd hushed.

"People of our planet," came the voice of the rocketeer, "we are saddened to inform you that God is a liar, a thief, and a murderer. He is fearful and

competitive and threatened. He exploits with his machines, and he doesn't care about the land."

An ocean of moans moved over the people. But they didn't mourn for the people of Earth. They didn't know to mourn for them.

They mourned because God was nothing liked they dreamed. They thought God was pathetic.

In the Christian story, humans are made in God's image (see "Question 5—Am I Valuable Enough?"). They are made to show the world (and each other) what God is like.

Humans have a mind, will, and emotion, just like God does. What a remarkable miracle, when you really think about it. It's right before our eyes. Most of the precious and valuable things about life are other people and our relationships with them.

We never give Nobel prizes to giraffes, but humanity pauses to celebrate the dedicated work of some, such as Wangari Muta Maathai, who bravely helped set people free.

What is so remarkable about humans? Could it be that the grand masterpiece of creation (humans) is yet another signpost of nature pointing us to its Source? Merely encountering other human beings serves as more evidence that God has spoken, more than anything else nature has produced.

Yet just like those aliens in the story discovered, sometimes we demonstrate God very badly. We are broken. We exploit others. We are fearful. Looking for God's image in us is like looking for our image in a shattered mirror. It's there, but it's twisted, fragmented, and warped.

God's image is still present in us, just as the mirror is still there. Yet it takes a lot more analysis to get a clear picture of who God is. It takes a lot of time to see what the shattered pieces are supposed to look like.

WRITTEN WORDS

The Christian God reveals himself most clearly and directly in the Bible.

If the New Testament's accounts are true, evidence for their truth must be clear. We shouldn't just announce, "The Bible is true because someone says so."

Many Christians are guilty of believing that the Bible is true because it says so in the Bible. Then they quote the verse.[61]

That explanation has never been helpful to me. Why? Even though my friend, Brian, may look like Superman doesn't mean he can go around saying, "I'm Superman because I say I'm Superman." Nobody will believe him. Many people will need more evidence than that. He may be Superman, and he may be right in saying so. But you need him to give more evidence than merely announcing it. Some eyewitnesses who can testify that they saw him lift his car above his head would help; even that they heard him break the sound barrier as he flew over their houses would do some good.

To learn whether or not the Bible is something we should take seriously and trust, first we should make sure it's reasonably true.[62] (Our focus will be on the New Testament because that contains the most crucial elements to glue together the whole story of the Bible.)

There are two things we need to understand first: ***preservation*** and ***reliability***.

Preservation means that *the New Testament we have today is what was originally written.* This would be similar to the preservation of bread—we want to eat it before mold and maggots find it. We want it preserved. In terms of the New Testament, we want to read it without the mold of later editing and tampering. We want it as close to the original text as possible.

Reliability means that *the New Testament we have today is telling the truth.* This would be similar to a friend showing up for dinner after he gave his word. We can trust him. Even if the *preservation* proves true for

---

[61] 2 Timothy 3:16-17, "All Scripture is God-breathed and is useful for teaching, rebuking, correcting and training in righteousness, so that all God's people may be thoroughly equipped for every good work."

[62] Notice I don't say "absolutely true." Remember the four "Special Rules" I mention in the Intermission section after chapter 3. I may not know something 100 percent, but that's not required for it to be *reasonable*. All I need is sufficient evidence, say 75 percent confidence, to satisfy me that something is more likely true than false.

the New Testament, it still could have been just a well-preserved lie. We want to find clues that prove it's trustworthy.

In order to trust an ancient document, both *preservation* and *reliability* are necessary. Without one or the other, the case for trusting the New Testament grows weaker.

(Note: At this point, we're not examining the Bible as a Holy Book. We're examining, comparing, and testing it just like all ancient books.)

The writers of the Bible really existed, just like you and me. And they really wrote, just like you and me. Just because some people highly respect the New Testament doesn't mean we can't put it to the same test as we do everything else. It wouldn't be fair to say that all books except the Bible may be analyzed and scrutinized. If the Bible is true, it will stand up on its own in light of the evidence. And we can only build real confidence in the Bible by standing on what we *find* to be true—not by standing on what we *want* to be true.

PRESERVATION

I once attended a rare-book show in Los Angeles where hundreds of vendors were selling their finest books.

For me, the highlight of the show was peering through the display glass at three large books. They were the final proof copies of J.R.R. Tolkien's *The Lord of the Rings*, bound in sculpted leather and with Elven writing around the edges. Inside, along the margins of the text, were Tolkien's own scribbled edits—his final touches before they became the legendary classics we know today.

I stared at them for a long time, taking in the handwriting of Tolkien and his imaginative stories.

We read Tolkien's works, and we're confident that what was written by Tolkien is what we read today. And even though the *Lord of the Rings* films altered some of the story, the heart and struggle of Middle-Earth is still captured on the silver screen.

Tolkien's writings have been *preserved*. We have the originals, and we know that what we read today is just as Tolkien wrote it.

But what will happen 1,000 years from now? Say a great fire burns all of Tolkien's original manuscripts, and most of the copies we have on our shelves today get donated after we die, and then other people read them and wear them out and toss them in the garbage because new editions had prettier covers.

One thousand years from now, people may begin to wonder if their copy of *The Lord of the Rings* contains the same text that Tolkien wrote. They may wonder if other Tolkien fans updated the books or added their own stories or made the characters wilder. People may begin to doubt whether the book is even worth reading because it may not be anything like the original.

Then let's suppose an archeological dig in your neighborhood turns up your copy of *The Lord of the Rings*. (You do have a copy, right?) The archeologist reports his findings that a copy of *The Lord of the Rings* was uncovered—one that was published only 50 years after the original. In reading it, they discover how close their own copies are to your copy. Even though they didn't have the original manuscript or a first edition of the book, having a copy published only 50 years after the original confirms what was edited and not edited in later centuries.

This would give people some really good evidence to believe that their copies of *The Lord of the Rings* are pretty close to the original version that Tolkien wrote.

We can apply this same idea to ancient writings, too.

LET'S COMPARE

Let's look at Plato, for example. Every important university in the country studies Plato. His *Republic* is considered one of the most important works on justice in Western civilization. Can Plato's work hold up under the test of *preservation*?

Plato wrote it around 400 BCE. Yet the earliest copy of his work is dated 900 CE. That's 1,300 years after it was written. And scholars know about only eight copies still in existence.

Look at the differences between Plato and the Tolkien example I gave above. It's reasonable to conclude that the chances of your Tolkien copy being accurate to the original are much greater than Plato's copies. Yet, Plato's views are taught in philosophy departments around the world, as though the copies are good enough.

Let's look at another ancient book called *The History of the Peloponnesian War* by Thucydides. Here we have a similar situation to Plato. The book was written around 430 BCE. Our earliest copy dates back to 900 CE. That's 1,300 years after it was written. How many copies do we have? We have eight.

Comparing Thucydides and Plato, we have little idea which one has been preserved more because we have so few copies to compare and so much time between the copy and the original. Yet Thucydides is consulted as one of the primary sources into ancient times.

What if we did the same test with the New Testament? What would we discover?

The writers of the New Testament wrote during the first century CE. The earliest copy we have is a fragment from the book of John dated around 117 CE. That's less than 50 years from the time it was written. We have copies of complete books of the New Testament from a hundred years after they were written. We have copies of the entire New Testament dating to 325.

The number of copies of the Greek New Testament still in existence total more than 5,000.

If we compare this information with Plato and Thucydides, the evidence is overwhelmingly in favor of the preservation of the New Testament, even more than the preservation of the celebrated works of Plato and Thucydides. The New Testament even has more evidence of its preservation than we do from our Tolkien illustration.

Something we should note is that one of the beliefs that founded the religion of Islam is the idea that the New Testament failed the test of preservation. Six hundred years after Jesus' time on earth, Muhammad claimed the New Testament was corrupted.

Yet the evidence doesn't lean in that direction at all. The evidence shows the heart of the New Testament *was not* corrupted. Who would know more about what Jesus said—those who listened at Jesus' feet, or someone who lived 600 years later when Muhammad lived? What does this evidence mean for the religion of Islam that requires—as its foundation—that the New Testament *was* corrupted? I'm not pointing this out to pick on Islam. I'm just offering this as something to consider in light of the claim that Islam makes.

TELEPHONE GAME

Some argue that you cannot know the preservation of anything, and they'll often use an example of the "telephone game" to show their point.

Remember playing the "telephone game" when you were in grade school? Everyone in the class sits beside one another. The teacher whispers something in one student's ear, like, "Bananas are yummy on cereal." That student then whispers what she heard to the student beside her. Down the line it goes, whispered from one to another and passed along. When the last student is told the message, he must recite it for the whole class: "Bungees," he says with a shrug of his shoulders, "warm laughing in yordle." The class erupts with laughter and everyone wants to play again.

Thus, some people use that example to say preservation is impossible because the message gets skewed every time.

That's not the way preservation works when it comes to books, however. Just like with our illustration of *The Lord of the Rings,* the book isn't whispered from one person to one another. It's written down on paper. And if you really like a quotation from Tolkien and want others to enjoy it, you'd go to the trouble of making sure your handwriting is neat and copying down all the phrases accurately. Then you'd pass the copied quote on to another.

That's how I'd replay the "telephone game" to demonstrate true preservation. I'd have the first student write down a phrase, and then pass the paper to the next student to copy it down in their neatest handwriting. Only, instead of using a boring phrase like "Bananas," I'd use something more rewarding, such as, "No homework for a month if you win the game!"

You can be sure every student would be nervous and careful not to let the whole class down. And writing it only doubly assures victory!

With the New Testament, not only was it written down, but it was also copied by hundreds of people at a time who were trained professionals. These copyists spent their entire lives meticulously copying the most important writings of the day. They'd go line by line, counting lines, counting letters and words. Their rechecking skills worked harder than the spellchecker on our computers today. And their motivation for maintaining accuracy was greater than having no homework assignments for a month. They were passing along the most sacred meanings of life.

That's not to say errors could not be made. But the chances of getting it right are hundreds of times greater than playing a round of the "telephone game." Plus, if one had unclear handwriting or skipped some lines, you still had hundreds of other copies to compare it with.

And if that wasn't enough, we also have letters and documents written by other people who lived at that time. And in those documents, the writers often quote the New Testament. So even if we only had those individual letters and documents, we'd still have enough quotations from the New Testament to reconstruct the New Testament. That'd be like starting the "telephone game" by sharing the message with a thousand people. And then those people would write about it in their emails and notes and homework papers. With all that evidence it might be harder to get the message wrong than get it right![63]

OLD IS USELESS?

Some mistakenly believe that just because something is old, it's also useless. However, just as we cannot judge a book by its cover, we cannot judge a book by its age. The real test is whether it's telling the truth, no matter how old or new that truth is. "The sun shines in the sky" is still true, even though it shone before history began. "Jesus is the Son of God," if true, is no less true in the Technology Age than it would have been true in the Iron Age. Truth has no expiration date.

Now if you understand all that, then you understand preservation. Do we have what was originally written now in the present day? I believe we

---

[63] This information on preservation can be gathered from many different sources. One I highly recommend for your bookshelf is *A General Introduction to the Bible* by Norman L. Geisler and William E. Nix.

do. We can apply that test to the writings of Tolkien, Plato, and Thucydides. And, as we've seen, we can also apply it to the New Testament.

RELIABILITY

Now just because we have lots of positive evidence that the New Testament has been well preserved, that doesn't mean the New Testament is true.

Suppose I write on a piece of paper that I went hang gliding in Brazil on September 17, 2006. I put that piece of paper in a time capsule with some other things to be uncovered 1,000 years from now.

Then on September 17, 3006, the capsule is opened. The people who open it find my "Most Improved" trophy from high school basketball, my first edition of C.S. Lewis' *The Great Divorce,* and a piece of paper that says something about hang gliding. Ooohs and aaahhs rise up from the gathered crowd. (Apparently, they really like my trophy!)

My piece of paper about hang gliding is in mint condition. It's the *original!*

Yet, does that mean it's true? No. The truth is I've never been hang gliding in my life, and on September 17, 2006, I ran the Disneyland Half Marathon with Jonalyn as a birthday present to her! So just because a statement has been preserved a long time, it isn't automatically true.

We need *reliability.*

TESTS OF RELIABILITY

What tests could we come up with that would allow us to know if someone were telling the truth?

TEST #1: MULTIPLE STORIES ABOUT THE SAME THING. I bungee jumped in New Zealand. Do you believe me? Maybe, if you know I'm the kind of person who doesn't lie about things like that. But how much more would you believe me if other people reported (testimony) seeing me bungee jump in New Zealand? Then it's very likely that I'm telling the truth.

The Bible applies this same rule in Deuteronomy 19:15 and Matthew 18:15, 16—to confront someone about something they've done wrong, you need two or three witnesses.

TEST #2: MY ENEMY SAID SOMETHING ABOUT ME THAT BENEFITED ME, BUT NOT MY ENEMY. Suppose I scored the highest in my class on a math test. I can tell you I scored the highest, and you might believe me. But how much more would you believe it, if my ruthless academic competitor told you? She may say it grudgingly, but she'd have no reason to say it if it weren't true. If she lied and said I scored better than the rest of the class, it would only serve to make her look worse. And it would also be weird for her to lie about something, which would make her appear less intelligent.

TEST #3: EMBARRASSING INFORMATION. I want people to like me, think well of me, and befriend me. I believe most people want that. Therefore, I would never want people to know about some things in my life because they might think I'm an embarrassment and reject me.

Here's an example. Suppose I attend a party. Someone else comes in and dangles a piece of information over my head. He hushes the group and announces that after I graduated from college, I stayed overnight at a friend's house and wet the bed. Everyone may laugh and will likely think this jerk is just making it up to make himself look better.

Yet, someone asks me, "Dale, is this true?"

If I admit it's true, then you'd probably believe me. Why? Because there'd be no reason to admit something embarrassing like that unless it was really true.

Scholars in the science of textual criticism use these three tests that I've just listed—*multiple stories, enemy stories,* and *embarrassing stories.* They also use many more, but for this section, I'll keep it to just these three so you can see how *reliability* offers a good case that the Bible is worth our trust.

I'll further narrow my focus by using these three tests on the most important event in Jesus' life: the empty tomb and Jesus being raised from the dead, also known as the "resurrection."

TEST #1: MULTIPLE STORIES ABOUT THE SAME THING

How many people wrote about the life of Jesus? Many have. People mention the life of Jesus not just in the Bible, but in other writings as well. There's no debate about whether or not Jesus lived. You'd have to ignore loads of evidence to say that he didn't.

Let's narrow down the question: How many people who actually *knew* Jesus or knew people who walked *closely* with Jesus wrote about the life of Jesus? Four that we know of (and with a reasonable amount of evidence). Their names are Matthew, Mark, Luke, and John. Collectively, their writings are also known as "the Gospels."

Matthew and John were students of Jesus himself. They heard and saw it all.

Mark was not a student of Jesus, so how do we know Mark's writings are true? Scholars believe he got the scoop from Peter. Peter was also a student of Jesus, just like Matthew and John. So Mark wrote down a lot of the things Peter told him.

Luke was not a student of Jesus either, but he did travel and speak with those who were. Luke writes like a journalist. He tells the reader in the first four verses of his book that he's writing an investigative report. And scholars note that Luke learned about the details of the Christmas story straight from the lips of Mary herself[54] (testimony), which is why we find the Christmas story detailed in Luke and not in any other writing about Jesus.

So of the four people in the New Testament who wrote about the life of Jesus, all of them either walked with Jesus (perception) or wrote down the information they heard from people who did (testimony). All the stories come from eyewitnesses. They weren't made up by some guy named "Billkinkat the Crazy Nut in Norway" centuries later. They were written by those who were present at the time when Jesus walked the earth. Think of their stories as separate books written by separate people, not as separate chapters in a larger book called "the Bible."[65]

---

[54] See the second chapter, "Question 2—What Is Truth?" and how "testimony" is a tool for knowing things.

[65] The Bible, both the Old Testament and the New Testament, is a collection of historical accounts, wise sayings, poetry, letters, future predictions, and biographies. All of those separate writings were compiled later. When thinking of the New Testament writings about Jesus, each book (Mathew, Mark, etc.) stands on its own and was only later put alongside the others because it was found to be deeply important to read, understand, and compliment the others.

All four of these writers report, among other things, the most significant event in the life of Jesus: his resurrection. All four of them said the tomb was empty, and Jesus is alive.

Sometimes antagonists say that the writers' accounts contradict each other. For example, one writer says there was only one angel at the empty tomb. Another one says there were two angels.[66] My question to them is this, "Does it matter to the overall story?"

It may matter if you're trying to defend that the Bible has no errors (which is not what I'm doing in this chapter). But it doesn't matter when it comes to the resurrection. Why?

Here's an example. A friend of mine was involved in a small auto accident. In the evening light, the police officer wrote down the wrong color car on the ticket. She reported it as being beige when it was actually silver. Before the judge, my friend pointed out this discrepancy. This irritated the judge.

"It was your car, right?" said the judge.

"Yes," my friend replied.

"Then the color written on the ticket doesn't matter. The issue today is an auto accident, not the precision of a color chart."

See the point? Even the writers, who may mention different numbers of angels, don't list a different number of tombs. One tomb had some sort of messenger of God waiting there. The same tomb was still missing Jesus' body. The same tomb was empty. And that's the point!

As we live with questions, in the Bible and in the rest of life, we must work hard at not getting bogged down with unnecessary details. After we get the point of the story, then we can struggle over the details.

All four writers report that the tomb is empty. And a fifth writer, named Paul, says 500 people saw Jesus after he rose from the dead. That's a lot of eyewitnesses!

So it passes the *test of multiple stories*. In scholarship, when you have two ancient witnesses of the same event, the event is considered likely. But when you have four witnesses, it renders the event nearly beyond doubt.[67]

---

[66] Compare Matthew 28 with Luke 24.

[67] From a lecture by Gary Habermas, Biola University, Fall 2004. Habermas attributes this phrase regarding multiple stories to scholar, Paul Maier.

Even so, just like our cumulative case for God's existence, we should evaluate the resurrection cumulatively as well. We must move on to test number two:

TEST #2: ENEMY STORIES

What do we find the enemies of Jesus saying about the resurrection? In Matthew 28:11-15, we read the report of how the guards ran to their superiors and told them what happened. Here's what it says:

> While the women were on their way, some of the guards went into the city and reported to the chief priests everything that had happened. When the chief priests had met with the elders and devised a plan, they gave the soldiers a large sum of money, telling them, "You are to say, 'His disciples came during the night and stole him away while we were asleep.' If this report gets to the governor, we will satisfy him and keep you out of trouble." So the soldiers took the money and did as they were instructed. And this story has been widely circulated among the Jews to this very day.

The guards were paid to lie and say the disciples had stolen the body to fool everyone.

The guards weren't watching the wrong tomb. They knew exactly where to stand and how to keep a trained soldier's eye on the place. There was no chance that a few fishermen, untrained in the art of war, could walk up behind them, silently roll away a gigantic boulder, and then steal Jesus' body under their watch.

I don't believe even Hollywood's special effects could pull that off.

In addition, the guards' superiors easily could have gone to the tomb to show it was the wrong one. They knew where it was located. It was the tomb of the rich man, Joseph of Arimathea. Joseph generously donated it so Jesus could have a respectful burial.

Yet neither the guards nor their superiors showed people were mistaken about the location of Jesus' tomb. Nor did they admit that Jesus rose from the dead. However, they *did* admit something important! They admitted the tomb was **empty** (perception). Here we have an enemy admitting the crucial evidence of the empty tomb, evidence that points in the direction of the resurrection of Jesus.

In the movie *The Body*, archeologists discover what they believe to be the tomb of Jesus. And inside that tomb, they discover a crucified body that, after further study, they believe to be the body of Jesus. He was never resurrected. When word gets out about what the archeologists found, the Catholic Church destroys the tomb for fear it will cause too much grief for people to learn the truth. One priest even commits suicide.

When I watched that movie, I kept wondering why everyone suddenly became afraid after this tomb was found.

I thought back to the evidences we have, including the enemy's stories. And if the movie was correct—that the body of Jesus *was* discovered—then there would need to be a lot of explaining done as to why the people who were there when it happened (or didn't happen) didn't produce the body themselves. We would need to know why the disciples made up a story they were willing to die for, why so many people claimed to see Jesus afterward, why the Christians formed a group that chose to meet on Sunday instead of the Jewish tradition of Saturday, and on and on.

I believe movie producers underestimate how the church would respond to such a discovery in light of so much evidence to the contrary.

The end of the movie reveals what the archeologists really discovered. But you'll need to watch it yourself to find out what it was. One hint: It wasn't the body of Jesus.

We've now passed two tests on the *reliability* of the story. Multiple stories about the same event weigh heavily. An enemy admitting the tomb was empty makes it even heavier. But what about the third test?

TEST #3: EMBARRASSING STORIES

If the story of the resurrection were made up to deceive humankind, then the writers certainly wouldn't include embarrassing stories that might hurt their credibility. Yet embarrassing stories are included throughout the different accounts.

For instance, take one of the most outspoken followers of Jesus who later became one of the loudest witnesses of the resurrection. His name was Peter. What did Peter do when Jesus told him he would go to Jerusa-lem and suffer and die in Matthew 16?

Peter confronted him, "Never, Lord! This shall never happen to you!"

And Jesus turns and confronts him, "Get behind me Satan! You are a stumbling block to me; you do not have in mind the concerns of God, but merely human concerns."

That's pretty embarrassing for well-intentioned-but-rash Peter.

Or look at Peter again in that famous scene in Matthew 26 when Jesus tells his students he's going to be tortured and killed and they will all scat-ter. Peter says, "Not me! I'm going with you to death."

I expect bravado from someone who's inventing a new religious order. But Jesus doesn't congratulate Peter, nor announce him as a great leader. Instead, Jesus tells him, "Peter, before the rooster crows, you will deny me three times."

And Peter does just that—publicly and with great protest—not once, but three times! And he even did so in response to a slave girl![68] (More on the ancient view of women later.)

That's very embarrassing behavior for one of the leading spokesmen of Jesus. So why would these details be included if the writers were simply making up the story of Jesus' resurrection? They hurt Peter's credibility, especially if he wants to convince people that his new religion is worth following.

At a recent event I spoke on a university campus, and a very skeptical graduate student approached me. We talked about embarrassing stories. He kept insisting, "How do we know they didn't put those embarrassing stories in there to use reverse-psychology to trick us into believing them?"

"First," I replied, "that would be weird. Second, I didn't embarrass myself or tell embarrassing stories about me when I was speaking tonight. And you still didn't believe me. What makes me think you'd believe me if I really said something to hurt my credibility?"

"I see your point," he said with a smile.

Let's take a brief look at the most often cited embarrassing moments surrounding the resurrection.

[68] Mark 14:27-31, 66-72.

In ancient days, women were not treated as they are in Western cultures today. Today, women are given full human status and the rights and privileges of citizenship capable of using mind, heart, and will for the good of others. In biblical times, women were not regarded so highly. In fact, it's documented that a woman's testimony in court was comparable to the testimony of a lying thief.[69]

That's what men thought of women. So if you're going to invent a story about the resurrection, then you'd better not make women important characters in the story. Their very presence would discredit you.

However, according to the *multiple stories* that were written about the resurrection, who are the first ones to discover the empty tomb? Women.[70] The story even says the disciples didn't believe the women.[71] That would be like putting the town drunk or a con man at the empty tomb. Those aren't credible witnesses. If you're inventing a story that you want others to believe, then you leave those guys out of it.

So what does the test of *embarrassing stories* teach us? That if the writers of the Gospels were lying about the resurrection, they would *not* have included information about all the blunders of Peter to possibly mess up his credibility and reputation. And they would *not* have put a couple of women at the empty tomb to be the first ones to share the story.

Therefore, the most likely explanation is this: They were telling the truth.

When we take a *cumulative* look at just these three tests, each gives us more evidence to know and have faith in the story of Jesus' resurrection.

Has God spoken? In the written word, the evidence is pointing hard to answer *yes*. Not only does the Bible's *preservation* line up, but also its *reliability* (whether or not it's telling the truth about the resurrection) is compelling.

And this is a very big deal. Later in this chapter I'll return to Jesus' resurrection and how it applies to God's speaking to us.

But has God spoken in other ways? Do we limit God's speaking only in nature and in written words? Since God created everything, including

---

[69] Talmud, Rosh Hashannah. For more discussion on the ancient view of women and the empty tomb, see Habermas and Licona, *The Case for the Resurrection of Jesus*.

[70] Matthew 28. Mark 16. Luke 24. John 20.

[71] Luke 24:11—"But they did not believe the women, because their words seemed to them like nonsense."

his written words, then everything is a potential tool for God to communicate. God has the freedom to choose whatever method of communication is sufficient for us to hear and understand what we *need* to hear and understand.[72]

GOD AS HIMSELF

In wondering if the God who is "out there" has actually spoken to reveal himself, I had to figure out whether nature and God's Word were actually pointing in the same direction.

And suddenly in history, something happens. John, who knew Jesus personally, wrote, "In the beginning was the Word...and the Word was God...Through him all things were made...and the Word became flesh and made his dwelling among us."[73]

Have you ever asked God this question—"God, if you're so real, why don't you just show up and say something?"

AND HE DID...

This is no joke. The God who created nature *became* nature. God became human, like us, and bridged the gap between him and nature. The God of the prairies came to earth in order to make himself the God of the church.

This is the focal point in all of history: God touches down. It's what theologians call the "incarnation." And in coming near to us, Jesus shows himself to be God in many different ways.

1) Jesus calls himself by the same titles that were used to refer to God in the Bible.

a. The Shepherd (Psalm 23; John 10)

b. The Light (Psalm 27:1; John 1:9)

---

[72] Some Christians protest this viewpoint and claim the Bible is the only way God speaks. But that doesn't fit with the Bible itself, which refers to God speaking through nature in Psalms 8 and 19. Plus, 2 Peter 1:3 says, "His divine power has given us everything we need for a godly life through our knowledge of him who called us by his own glory and goodness." God's "divine power" is all we need and it can be communicated to us through everything that belongs to God—which is everything!

[73] John 1:1, 3, 14.

2) Jesus forgives sins, which only God can do.

3) Jesus allows himself to be worshiped as God, which is ungodly to allow, unless you're God.

4) Jesus heals the sick, raises the dead, and even conquers death itself.

Jesus is God in disguise. God came near enough for us to see him, yet God clothed himself in skin and became a human so we wouldn't be overwhelmed by seeing him in his purity and power in full force. Remember what I noted earlier: God will choose a way that is *near enough* to affirm our minds and hearts, but at the same time still *far enough* not to overwhelm us.

Here's an important point that links us back to the beginning of this chapter on whether or not God has spoken in his written Word. Does Jesus know what he's talking about?

IS JESUS QUALIFIED?

If you've been skimming along so far, this is the point in the book when you really want to pay attention. It's likely the most important point in these pages.

If Jesus rose from the dead, then he is the *only* person who has lived on both sides of reality—physical and spiritual—and lived to tell about it. He has the credentials.

Jesus *does* know what he's talking about, so we should pay close attention.

Jesus had no problem believing in the Bible, and he quoted from it often. If Jesus is indeed God, then that means Jesus even wrote the Bible from which he's quoting. When I get people objecting to whether the whale swallowed Jonah, I don't point to ancient Nineveh as evidence. I first point to Jesus who had no problem believing it either.[74] Of all people, I believe Jesus may be the only One who knows what he's talking about when it comes to the ultimate meaning of life.

Jesus doesn't just give us truth. He calls himself the Truth.[75] He talks as if he's the source from which all other truths flow.

[74] Matthew 12:40.
[75] John 14:6.

Jesus is the only One who knows for sure that God has spoken. And in Jesus, God has spoken through himself.

The writer of Hebrews says the same thing: "In the past God spoke to our ancestors through the prophets at many times and in various ways, but in these last days he has spoken to us by his Son, whom he appointed heir of all things, and through whom also he made the universe" (Hebrews 1:1-2).

I believe the Wiccans get it half-right. There is something coming through nature that is powerful and affirming. Yet there is something more: the One behind nature. In Jesus we have the Author of nature, who created it for our home, and who became part of it so we can know him better. It's like a playwright entering his own play.

Do you see the deeper meaning of this? This means God finds us humans valuable enough to become one of us. God entered history to make himself known, to show that nature is good and important, and to make nature capable of knowing him. If you want to know what God is like, look to Jesus. God has come.

This is why Christmas is supposed to be such a dramatic celebration. But the very thing we humans want—for God to come near and tell us how to know him—we've managed to turn into a shopping spree that's covered in garland, trees, tinsel, twinkling lights, and hot foamy drinks.

God has come near—and we sing about reindeer and snow.

THE SILENCE OF GOD

It would be a mistake to ignore the fact that there are two sides to this question of whether or not God has spoken. And both sides are important.

One side is the theoretical. This is all the information we need in order to understand the ways God has spoken. And sometimes it's tedious. Yet the tediousness is hard work that we all need to put in if we care about the question and want confidence in the answer.

The other side is a matter of experience. "Has God spoken?" quickly becomes "Is God speaking now? Where is God? Why can't I feel him?"

God's silence is troubling. It shakes us. The words, "God may have done miraculous things in the past, but what is he doing in our lives now?" haunt me when I cannot write down what God is doing right now. Sometimes I just don't know.

And life grows difficult. Friends betray us. Girlfriends or boyfriends break up with us. Our parents divorce. We need money, but we don't know where to get it. Family members become sick. Someone we love dies.

The suffering gets harder to take when God is silent. We may want to shout or sing to scream out all of our emotions, just to see if God will speak to us through our feelings. But we also want to be careful we don't pretend our emotions and God's voice are the same things.

We want God to be near, but we have to remember there's a difference between God's nearness and my *feeling* his nearness. Since God is always present, it's difficult to say God *isn't* near. But I don't always feel him. And that troubles me.

One student writes, "*Can it be okay that I can't always feel God? Is it okay that God sometimes feels far away, even if I haven't done anything wrong?*"

That's a question I have to live with myself. And it's a question you and I will have to live with our whole lives as we grow to understand who we are and how God loves us.

One thing that helps me is looking at Jesus. He faced darkness. He knew his arrest was coming in a matter of moments. So he went into a garden in Jerusalem, and he deeply prayed for his Father to hear his prayer. In essence, this is what he prayed:

> *If it be your will, let this cup of suffering and death pass from me. I do not want to drink it. I do not want to be a sacrifice and shoulder the sins of the world.*
>
> *Yet regardless, I want your will and not my own.*

Isaiah aptly described Jesus as the "man of sorrows."[76] Jesus was betrayed by a close friend; all of his students ran away; and then he was unfairly treated, unjustly tried, and executed by the government.

[76] Isaiah 53:3.

Even more so, Jesus was deeply frightened by something else. He knew he was about to shoulder all the evils of humanity—every genocide, crime, sexual slavery, deceit, betrayal, and twisted thing. And in this moment, his Father would turn his back on Jesus. For the first and only time in existence, the love of the Trinity had something come between them. And that, more than anything, was what Jesus wanted to avoid.

He cried, "My God, my God, why have you forsaken me?"[77]

Jesus knew his Father's silence, too.

For those hours after he died, Jesus was separated from his Father so that you and I wouldn't have to be separated from God. Jesus made a way for us to never have to experience God's silence permanently.

As songwriter Andrew Peterson put it,

> When the questions dissolve into the silence of God,
> The aching may remain, but the breaking does not.

Even though we may ache and weep when God is silent and when some of our questions go unanswered, we can ultimately rest knowing God hasn't turned his back on us. This, too, shall pass.

When I find myself wondering where God is or whether God cares, I have to go back to realizing how God acts in history. We see this in God's written words, and we see this in the incarnation of Jesus. I need to be reminded of how God revealed himself in the past so I can be mindful of God in the present.

And when I find God is silent, my task is to keep doing the things before me, such as loving other people, mowing my lawn, and doing my work well. Perhaps there is growth to be had in being willing to do good even when it doesn't feel very important.

God's silence may be just for a time or a season in our lives, and it may happen for many different reasons. But it isn't permanent for those who seek God. And we can be confident that God is near, even when we can't feel him. Sometimes we have to stand on what makes sense, even when our circumstances or our emotions aren't cooperating.

[77] Matthew 27:46; Mark 15:34.

GOD HAS SPOKEN

Look at the dramatic and confident ways God has done exactly that.

• God has given us nature. This way of speaking to us is so powerful that some people even worship it, mistaking the creation for the Creator. And in nature, the special creation of humans shows us there is something magical going on outside of nature.

• God has given us specific words in his written Word. These words can even be verified to be reliable.

• God has given us…God! The God of eternity showed up in Time. The Infinite became finite so we can know the Infinite. God's love became hands and feet to heal and forgive and give us something nature never could: Good life that never ends.

In the previous chapter, I mentioned that love only makes sense when you have a Trinity, and that Christianity is the only worldview that holds this view. Now we can see more clearly that this loving, life-giving Trinity is concerned about us—concerned enough to speak.

This is by no means the last word on the evidence. It only scratches the surface. This is only the beginning of understanding God's interaction with us. These are signposts to look at, consider, explore, and grow into. This is a direction to walk into the meaning of things.

And this gives us confidence to hold on in the times when God is silent. We cannot demand how and when God speaks, but we can hold on with gratitude that God has given us enough evidence to know he is there.

Our response now is to **listen**.

QUESTIONS TO LIVE INTO

Spend some time alone in nature. Are you the kind of person who feels something "spiritual" about nature? What is God telling you *through* nature? Journal about it.

Do you have a hard time accepting history as fact? Do you have a hard time believing that old things can be as true as new things? If so, why?

Why does embarrassing evidence help boost the credibility of the resurrection account?

Does some of the evidence in this chapter for the preservation and reliability of the Bible help answer some of your questions? If not, what's your next question? Write it down. Are you willing to search for the answer? If not, what's stopping you?

Purchase *The Case for the Resurrection of Jesus* by Gary R. Habermas and Michael R. Licona and read chapters 1 and 2.

Notes

_____

_____

_____

_____

_____

QUESTION 5

AM I VALUABLE ENOUGH?

In her bedroom with the door locked, Genny felt between her mattresses for her hidden razor blade. She never wanted to kill herself. No, that would be too dramatic, too crazy. She just wanted to feel something, anything that would melt some of the numbness within her.

Her best friend knew about the cutting and asked her to stop.

"Will you stop for me?" she asked.

Genny looked at her. "It isn't about you."

"So? I just don't want you to do it. It hurts you. Will you stop for me?"

"That reason isn't enough," replied Genny. She stared down at the curb. Then turned back to her house, tugging at her long sleeves, which she wore all summer long.

Speaking to a group of students at a camp in California, Jonalyn and I shared about cutting. I read a story written by a 13-year-old, whom we'd met during our travels, who struggled with the same thing. When I finished the short story, two teenagers in the audience were shaking and sobbing.

After everyone was dismissed, Jonalyn listened to their stories. They added an important comment:

> We hear speakers all the time at school and church and wherever. They talk about sex and drugs and alcohol and other typical things for teenagers. We don't struggle with those things. Many of us don't struggle with that. But no one has ever talked about cutting...until today.

There are many things that make students "cut," and they rarely have anything to do with suicide. Yet of the many reasons students give, there is one that shows up frequently. And this particular thing doesn't lead only to cutting. It also influences many other issues, from eating disorders to clothing choices to plastic surgery.

When I ask students to write down their questions, many sound like this:

> How come I don't feel like I'm worth anything?
>
> Is there something special about me?

Why would God love me?

Am I valuable if I'm not attractive?

BOMBARDMENT

People living in America are bombarded with images of sexiness. Even against our will, we see billboards and newsstands displaying eye candy and bodies for sale. These images affect us all. Companies know our deep need to feel valued in the Wild. And they know how quickly we'll throw our money at beauty products or magazines if they use images of beautiful men and women to lure us in.

So companies keep using people. "Sex sells" is a slogan that businesses have exploited for many decades. And it's why Hugh Hefner, the founder of *Playboy*, has all the money he could ever spend.

No doubt this has deep consequences for all who live in the Wild and are often lured by diversions (see the first chapter for a list of diversions, "Question 1—Does What I Think Really Matter?").

THE MEASURING STICK

It gives us a measuring stick of comparison.

For example, women compare themselves with the images of sexy women used in advertisements. These images are a judgment—not a mirror—even when the magazines don't say anything about *your* particular inadequacy. Even still, the ads and magazine articles often promise to help you become more like the pictures of the women you see: "10 tips to improve your eyes," "Five ways to slim down for summer," etc.

We're susceptible to believing these statements and promises because we care so deeply about what others think about us, and we want to be accepted.

Men are not exempt from these kinds of comparisons. Many men at the gym aren't looking to strengthen their bodies for their jobs, but to look more attractive than other guys and more alluring to women. They compare themselves with one another and with male models, too.

When I entered junior high, it was the first time I took physical education as a class. Throughout elementary school, recess offered plenty of exercise for me, with our pick-up games of dodge ball or relay races. But in junior high, the games became more coordinated. And we had to learn how to take care of our bodies.

Part of the new hygiene regiment involved group showers. This was torture for a kid going through puberty. Everyone goes through that awkward stage of life at different speeds. I wasn't part of the biologically accelerated program. And what made it worse was the fact that the upperclassmen were in the same showers with us. Awkwardly, we'd all undress, while our teacher watched to make sure we all got thoroughly drenched.

Hurriedly, I'd throw off my clothes and toss my towel on the rack near the showers. Then taking great care not to look at anyone else below the waist, I'd take a quick shower and dart for my towel again.

Public showers are humiliating. I learned that in many schools, the girls' locker room had individual shower stalls while the guys still had to use the large, open shower room. *Why the difference? Is there something about women looking at women that's worse than men looking at men?*

I found that inconsistent. And to this day, I still believe public showers are inappropriate. In that room of nakedness, comparisons happen instantly. And inadequacies are developed and nurtured.

Guys are notorious for acting tough to cover up their insecurities. They bully each other. They talk big. They insult other guys in front of the girls. And the ones who do it the most are usually the ones who feel the most insecure. (I wish I'd known about that back in high school and college!)

It's one of those ironies in life—the tougher we try to sound, the more likely it is that we're just covering up a deeper weakness. You rarely hear the star player of the game announce that he's the best. He just proves it out on the field. It's the mediocre players, the ones who are insecure about their status, who make the self-proclaimed announcements.

CHANGING OUR TASTES

Another consequence of our bombardment by sexy images is that they change our tastes. They create new appetites and a new measuring stick by which to compare our future boyfriends and girlfriends. In the old days, for example, a man may see a dazzlingly attractive woman only once in his lifetime. So he learned to develop a broader taste and definition of beauty, and he found a lovely bride right in his own village.

Today, men see all the most dazzling beauties from all the villages around the world. There is little chance of finding that girl on the billboard because she's already taken. But even still, the standard has been made. The definition of beauty becomes the narrow range of perfectly symmetrical skinny-mini models plastered on billboards.

I recently spoke with a father of grown children, and we talked about the power of pornography. He admitted it wasn't the nudity that captured his attention. It was the engaging, provocative eyes of the woman in the picture. It was her captivating gaze that seemed to be only for him. We all long to be looked at in that way.

Yet that gaze appears in more than just pornography. The stare of longing appears in regular magazines, advertisements, billboards, and even movies.

Girls struggle with visual stimulation, too. A few years ago, I was with some friends in an Abercrombie store. As we walked out, one of the girls commented about the pictures of the guys on the walls.

"It does something to me down there," she said.

I tried to pretend it wasn't a big deal that she'd said that, even though I was surprised to learn that girls are sexually moved by images of men. It revealed something that many weren't talking about—something true about the way sexy images affect us. Many people believe the messages in those images and allow them to exploit us.

I have a friend who's almost 50 years old, and he has journeyed through nearly every side of the Wild. He's found that women are often more sexually charged and explicit than men. While men are usually blamed for being sexual aggressors, feminine sexuality is too easily overlooked and ignored. Therefore many women respond by going even farther over the line to prove they're sexually aggressive, too.

Men and women both have sexual needs that are gifts from God. And our desires are easily awakened, just as the waft of fresh waffles makes us hungry—even after a big lunch.

SCREWTAPE'S STRATEGY

C.S. Lewis writes about the ability to manipulate our visual tastes. In his book *The Screwtape Letters,* Lewis writes about a junior devil named Wormwood who receives letters from his uncle, a senior devil named Screwtape.

In these letters, Screwtape gives his nephew lots of advice for the devices of excellent tempting. Screwtape writes,

> *It is all a fake, of course; the figures in the popular art are falsely drawn; the real women in bathing suits or tights are actually pinched in and propped up to make them appear firmer and more slender and more boyish than nature allows a full-grown woman to be. Yet at the same time, the modern world is taught to believe that it is being 'frank' and 'healthy' and getting back to nature. As a result we are more and more directing the desires of men to something which does not exist—making the role of the eye in sexuality more and more important and at the same time making its demands more and more impossible. What follows you can easily forecast!*[78]

In short, the eye gets used to seeing women in a certain way, and clothing props and creates intentionally slimming cuts and tricks of the eye. And the more we manipulate our bodies to get the shapes we desire, the more unnatural those lines become. Soon we'll find we want things we cannot have because what we want doesn't even exist.

It's quite obvious this has already happened with the sexy marketing images of men and women. Yet it's gone beyond that. Take the Victoria's Secret "Wonderbra." Why is it a wonder? Because it pushes and prods the breast to make it appear perpetually up and out. The real shape, the one God made, is manipulated.[79]

What happens in the honeymoon bed, when the Wonderbra is removed? How does he react to reality? Does she now feel insecure? Did they ever consider what God may have intended for them through sexual expression?

[78] C.S. Lewis, *The Screwtape Letters.*

[79] By the way, have you thought about the store name, "Victoria's Secret"? The Victorian era was when Queen Victoria ruled England during the late eighteenth century. It was a time when talk about sex was thought inappropriate. So when the modern-day store takes the name "Victoria's Secret," it's pulling back the curtain to reveal everything it can about sex. It's a clever wordplay on historical attitudes.

It's a tragic when diversions change our tastes in bodies and people—especially when those new tastes have nothing to do with reality.

THE OBSESSION

Where does this lead us? For some it doesn't lead much of anywhere. Some understand the lies of the images and work hard at ignoring them. But for others it becomes an obsession with appearance. Sensual photographs of men and women all work against the important thing.

Short story writer, Ray Bradbury writes about a man who makes a Happiness Machine. This machine is filled with all sorts of movies and images from other countries, as well as the smells from fields and Paris perfumes. It delivers many pleasures to the user from all around the world.

When the Happiness Machine is complete, the builder asks his wife to climb inside to test it. At first she laughs and then "oohhhs" and "aahhhs." Then she begins to cry. The inventor turns off the machine.

"What's wrong?" he asked. "You are crying. You are not supposed to be crying in a Happiness Machine!"

His wife cleared the tears from her eyes. "In your machine, you had me dancing. We haven't danced in 20 years."

"I will take you dancing tomorrow night!" her eager husband said.

"No, no. It's not important. It shouldn't be important. But your machine tells me it's important, and so I believe. The machine says, "You're young." I'm not. It lies, that Sadness Machine."[80]

Do you see what happened? The images we face, especially when they're bigger than life and appealing to our senses, often tell us what's important, even without using any words.

And that's the crazy thing about images these days, especially in the Wild. First, images get our attention. Then they appeal to our senses—they make us feel good. And before long, we really enjoy those images.

[80] Science Fiction Theatre, Ray Bradbury's *The Happiness Machine*.

Our tastes change. We look forward to seeing them again. We crave them, and then we compare ourselves to them.

Before we even realize it, we let those images tell us what's important, who to be, and what we need to become. Then our beliefs change, and we form new desires. We even start to make choices based on our new beliefs and desires.

We become objects of each other, to look at, crave, and enjoy. Then we become objects of ourselves, looking in the mirror, searching for our identity in our appearance.

If we cannot imitate the newest images in *Sports Illustrated, Seventeen, Abercrombie, People,* or *Cosmo,* we're discouraged and troubled.

We're reminded that we're lost.

Images go from being merely pictures on paper to value judgments in our souls. They tell us whom and what we need to fix in order to fit in.

IMAGE IN *THIRTEEN*

A powerful movie about the pressures students face is *Thirteen.* A girl named Tracy is confronted with a new era of life: the teenage years. In her struggle to fit in, she starts to imitate Evie, the popular, sexy girl in school—the one all the guys notice.

Then the story starts to unravel. Tracy wants to be part of Evie's group, so she changes her wardrobe, learns to steal, and experiments with sex and drugs. But all the while, Tracy is unhappy, and she starts cutting herself.

Nikki Reed, who plays Evie and also cowrote the script, makes it clear that the drugs, sex, rebellion, cutting, and stealing all hinge on one thing:

> *Nikki said the movie isn't intended as a shocking wake-up call for adults; it's simply a glimpse of life at a West Los Angeles middle school where drugs, sex and self-destruction are part of the daily routine.*
>
> *In hindsight, though, Nikki said the most damaging part of a 13-year-old's life isn't any of those things that parents worry about. Instead, it's the obsession young girls have with their appearance.*[81]

[81] *Miami Herald,* "'Thirteen' star is a reluctant spokeswoman" by Samantha Critchell, August 30, 2003. http://ae.miami.com/entertainment/ui/miami/movie.html?id=111838&reviewId=12954

Nikki admits what many suspect but rarely talk about. It's a personal struggle, and it makes us awkward, create excuses, and cover up. Personal struggles have that effect. Better off talking about major problems—such as drugs or suicidal tendencies. That way we don't feel so bad about ourselves.

However, obsession with our appearance is a powerful influence over other areas of life. It's no surprise that a common gift of choice in South Orange County high schools is either a new car or breast implants.

WHO WILL LOVE ME?

Obsession over our appearance nails us in the dating world. Many questions confront us during our teenage years about whom we'll marry.

While waiting for a doctor's appointment recently, I thumbed through the magazines on the rack in the waiting room. I found an issue of *Seventeen* that included a series of articles about young women learning to accept their physical imperfections. One had a scar on her face from an accident when she was a toddler. She opted not to do cosmetic surgery because the scar makes her unique. Another girl's face is covered with deep freckles. She hated them when she was younger, but now she realizes they make her one-of-a-kind and are a natural form of makeup.

These are the kinds of articles that need to be written because they offer us new perspectives on dealing with real beauty. Hats off to *Seventeen* for publishing them.

But then the opposite message is told. In the same issue, they boast more than 700 tips on how to be sexier. This includes wearing longer shirts to lengthen the torso, certain sleeves to thin the arms, shirts that broaden the shoulders, and skinny jeans that accent the legs. If people take the other articles seriously, then these 700 tips shouldn't mean very much.

That contradiction was bad enough, but then I flipped to a section that made me angry. It was the message from the male population. One page had a list of products, from lipstick to dresses, and under each item was a quotation from a guy. Jeff (age 21) tells girls what he likes about lip gloss. Brian (age 15) shares what he likes about dresses.

Do you see the problem? Now the unfortunate reader of *Seventeen* is given the impression that Jeff, Brian, and others represent the opinions of *all* guys her age. And now lodged in her mind are these false beliefs or little curses that will follow her as she makes decisions about her appearance. If she wants a guy like Jeff, she'd better wear that perfume he likes, or wear that dress. She may not even realize that Jeff isn't the guy she really wants. What she really wants is a guy who is sick of the games girls play—the games they've learned from reading *Seventeen* magazine. But how is she to know? This is her only source for "insider information" into the mysterious world of men.

It's easy to see why she believes her appearance becomes her only virtue—and a way to attract men she doesn't even want. But she believes, and she buys.

The diversions go deeper and now she's further adrift in the Wild.

LOVE

Love isn't found in "catching" a guy. Women weren't made for that. Love is in humility and respect. It's in vulnerability.[82] (I know it's a dreaded word—but essential.) It's in honor.

Sexiness is merely a dash of cinnamon on a brownie, not the whole mix of a woman. Besides the fact that you cannot sell sexiness; you can only sell clothing or perfume.

If you find a guy by making him long for your sex appeal, then you've found a guy who'll only emphasize those desires when he's with you. If you're always flirting with guys, you're only setting yourself up for shallow relationships. And this habit won't stop once you marry.

Good guys aren't drawn to girls who make a habit of flirting. Good guys are looking for intimacy. And intimacy draws two lovers into an exclusive privacy of the inner self that's shared with no one else.

If you're a guy who finds your value by rescuing a damsel in distress, you may find you've only attached yourself to a distressed woman. If you find fulfillment by trying to be the hero to your woman, then you may find yourself falling off your own pedestal.

---

[82] See Jonalyn Grace Fincher, *Ruby Slippers: How the Soul of a Woman Brings Her Home,* for a refreshing discussion on the virtues of feminine vulnerability.

We need to do better than these alternatives offered in the Wild. We need a place to be ourselves, to have value, and to find love. We need a little bit of Home in our relationships.

APPEARANCE AND OUR WORTH

Why is appearance so important to us?

Because how we appear often determines our worth in others' eyes. It's the same in *Thirteen* as it is in real life. It's an idea we grow to believe in our world.

So we keep up our appearances in every way we can. We'd better do what others do to fit in. We'd better do what it takes to be valuable.

It's no surprise that the question, "Am I important enough?" is common among students. It haunts most of us. It haunts me.

SELF-DISAPPROVAL

When I was a kid, I had tons of freckles. I remember looking in the mirror when I was 11, and I hated the way I looked. I hated my teeth. I hated my hair. I felt ugly, unattractive, unwanted. I thought no girl would ever want to date a guy like me. Then my mom would come over and pull out the brush and mess with my hair. "That's my handsome son!" she'd say.

Nice try, I thought. *But that's what moms are* supposed *to say.*

The desire to be attractive, and therefore valuable, never went away. I disapproved of myself as long as I thought I was unattractive.

WHAT MAKES US VALUABLE?

But who said attraction was connected to value? What makes us valuable? If we can discover that, we can live our questions into some answers.

I figure the best way to discover the value of something is to go back to how it was made.

Violins are valuable because they can make beautiful music. But not all violins are equally valuable. A Stradivarius is more valuable than ones you'll find in your local high school symphony. A Stradivarius is made of multiple woods and through special techniques used by the master crafts-man, Antonio Stradivari, to create the purest violin sound ever. I've seen the only complete quartet of Stradivari's stringed instruments on display in Madrid. In 2006, a Stradivari violin sold at auction for more than $3.5 million. That's one amazing violin.

So let's do the same thing for humans. What clues do we have about the creation of humans that make us valuable? Was there a Stradivari-like craftsman involved? What did he really make?

A man named Moses is one of the most famous characters in history. Moses talked with God, and he penned the story about the creation of humans. This story had been part of his people's history for generations, and it was important enough to preserve.

So Moses wrote it down, and you can read it for yourself in Genesis 1 and 2. "In the beginning God created the heavens and the earth." That's how the story starts. It's the beginning of the universe, our world included.

God populates the heavens with the sun, moon, and stars. God populates the earth with all sorts of living creatures, including birds, fish, and animals.

Then on the last day spent making the multifaceted aspects of our world, God decides to make something completely unique. This would be the crown of creation for the Earth (and as far as we know, the crown of the universe). God decides to make creatures like himself.

"Let us make human beings in our image," said God. Moses writes that God scooped up some earth and breathed into it. Suddenly, a unique creature was made. A human suddenly appeared for the first time ever on the planet. A human became "a living being."[83]

Genesis says God created the man first, and then the woman. Does that mean men are more valuable than women? No more than a sunrise is more valuable than a sunset. They are different but both equally valuable.

What you may not have noticed is that Genesis chapters 1 and 2 tell the same story in two different ways. Genesis 1 is like a summary. Genesis 2 simply fills in the details.

So what does Genesis 1:27 say?

[83] Genesis 2:7.

So God created human beings in his own image,

in the image of God he created them;

male and female he created them.

Who was made in God's image? Humans, both male and female. Both were equally valuable, and they both had a job to bear God's image together. It apparently took two different genders to make the complete image of God on earth the way God wanted it to be.

This is our origin, forged in an ancient age in the Garden of Eden, from the dust of paradise and the very breath of God. The Grand Artist, far superior to Stradivarius himself, crafts his ultimate artwork into his image. God makes humans.

In our origin comes our value.

A STORY IN THE WILD

Yet what's the alternative in the Wild today? Many say the story of our origin is aligned with atheistic evolution. Public education says we're mysteriously crafted by random particles that happened to converge on our planet. And these happened to develop complexity and emerge living organisms that eventually became humans. There is nothing in our existence that is purposed or important. We're only valuable because we say we're valuable or because we can outsmart and manipulate the rest of creation.

If this story is right, it's quite consistent to say (as one university professor once said) that an adult dog may be more valuable than a newborn human baby. Atheistic evolution finds value in function. If you can fetch the morning paper, you're more valuable than someone who can't.

In God's story, value comes from *who* made you and how he made you, regardless of what you can do.

Without purpose being given to us from outside of creation, it's difficult to see why value is important anyway. Who invented the label "valuable" and who says what's valuable? If value is invented from within ourselves, then who said our opinions of ourselves are valuable? And who says our opinions of our opinions of ourselves are valuable? And why aren't animals or rocks or clouds just as valuable as we are? And why is life more valuable than non-life?

If our origin has to invent value in order to tell us about value and who is valuable, what does that tell us about our own value? Do we even have it?

If value is invented, why do our souls cry out for it, and why do we look for it with desperation? Could it be that we're more than atheistic evolution is letting us be?

Again, the Christian story validates some of our deep longings that we can't erase just because some people in modern education try to do so. The Christian story comes through with a profound explanation of our importance and gives us a status as creatures far above anything in the Wild can invent. We're all—men and women—made in God's image, and we're designed with the power of reason and imagination and love.

We are more than picture-images of what everyone else wants us to be.

We are *God's* images who are designed to be ourselves.

WHAT DOES *GOD'S IMAGE* MEAN?

But what does it mean to be "made in God's image"?

My wife sat through a lecture at a large public university where the teacher shared his view of "God's image."

"The Bible says that humans were made in God's image," he said. "Does that mean God has armpit hair?" The class erupted with laughter, while the Christians in the class who took the value of humans seriously sat still feeling embarrassed.

This professor was unfair, and here's a simple illustration to explain why.

You've seen pennies before. Whose image is on the penny? Abraham Lincoln. That's not controversial.

Yet there are some things that are true about the penny that are not true about Abraham Lincoln. For instance, what's a penny made of? Copper. Does that mean Abraham Lincoln was made of copper? No. What size is a penny? It's about three-fourths of an inch in diameter. Is Abraham Lincoln that small? No.

I cannot judge this professor's motives for beating up the Bible in front of his students. But I can judge his conclusion. An "image" is not a "reproduction." When God made us in his image, he did not make a reproduction of himself. God simply made us in special ways like he is.

There are different opinions on how we're made in God's image. I'll share my view with you. When the Bible talks about the "long arm of the Lord," it's poetic language about his quality of character. God is willing to go a long way to reach out to us. God doesn't really have arms. God does not have a body. God is not made of matter. Yet when God made us in his image, he put some things in us that are like things in him.

God has a soul. God has a mind, emotions, and a will. God thinks, feels, and chooses. And because of these abilities, God loves, creates, and enjoys others. When we were made in God's image, we were given characteristics unique to any other creature in the galaxy. Genesis 2:7 says we became a living being. We were made one part body (which God does not have) and one part soul (which God does have). We were given a mind, will, and emotions. We can love others, create art, and enjoy God and life.

This is amazing. We are made in the image of the High King. We reflect what God is like. We are princes and princesses in the world from our very beginning.

This is one of the great themes of the whole Bible: Know God and show the world what God is like by being a whole human being. You're made in God's image. Apart from what you do, what you look like, or what other people think of you, you have value in your very being.

REMOVING DIGITAL MANIPULATION ISN'T ENOUGH

One manufacturer of skin care products, Dove, started a campaign to curb the problem of appearance obsession. Their commercial (seen on YouTube) shows an ordinary woman going to a photo shoot. Her pictures are then manipulated on a computer and put up on a billboard. The picture on the billboard only slightly resembles the real model, but the public sees a picture of a beautiful woman they can emulate.

Dove is trying to pull back the curtain on the manipulation that goes on in advertising. They want to help curb the eating disorders and other issues that come with girls worrying about their appearance. But are they successful?

Only time will tell. Dove's new campaign shows pictures of teenage girls without makeup. I've seen these pictures in store displays. Yet I predict this new campaign won't curb the struggle many people have with their appearance.

On the one hand, Dove has found *real* beautiful women for their advertising campaign—women who don't need digital manipulation or makeup. Many women believe it's hard enough to keep up appearances *with* makeup. But if people start judging you for wearing makeup, then there's *no* chance to hide the appearances we've learned to despise.

On the other hand, there's something deeper going on. While Dove wants to help women to some degree, they still want to make more money. And people will still believe appearance equals value.

Here's the deeper problem—Dove is still using or objectifying women to sell their products. The image of God in women is exploited so some investors can sell soap. Women in advertising, with or without makeup and with or without Photoshopped images, are still dominating the standard all women must attain. It's still shaping our tastes of what's beautiful and what's valuable. It still praises the body and shrinks the soul.

Could it be that people aren't supposed to be treated as objects for marketing purposes? Could it be that by making images of people larger than life, we've also shrunk down some of the value and dignity of life?

The problem is not manipulated images on the billboard. The problem has more to do with objectifying people with images. The problem is when we stop seeing people as image bearers of God.

GROWING TO BELIEVE

It's not saying girls shouldn't be wearing makeup. It's not about changing our advertising methods from manipulated images of beautiful women to unmanipulated images of beautiful women.

We must get back to remembering whose image we bear.

And we must grow to believe it as true.

IS IT REALLY TRUE?

The reason many Christian students still struggle with their image, even after they've heard they've been made in the image of the God, is because they don't really believe it's true. They still collect the magazines filled with beauty secrets. They still spend large amounts of time in front of the mirror. Yet they don't know why they still struggle with it.

It's because we will believe what we spend our time thinking about. And our beliefs will determine the kind of person we become. If we believe our appearance makes us valuable, then we become a person obsessed with appearance.

Of course, it's too simple to say the heart of the problem is advertising. The problem comes to us in many ways that affect our beliefs. Another one of those beliefs is the way men and women interact. One assumption generally believed today is that men pursue beautiful women; therefore, women have to be beautiful to be pursued by men.

This is a problem that has gone on for centuries. It tells women they must be preoccupied with their appearance to get a guy. And that reinforces our belief that appearance will bring value and value will bring love.

As long as we play romantic cat and mouse based on our appearances, we'll continue to shape our beliefs in a way that's contrary to the miracles and mysteries that created us. Some of the most attractive women I've been privileged to know were not the stereotypically glamorous. It was something about their souls, something that Victoria Secret could never market.

WHAT OUR QUESTIONS REALLY MEAN...

As we live with our questions, sometimes we come to understand what our questions really mean. What is the real desire behind the question, "Am I valuable enough?"

Even though we are made in the image of God, that doesn't seem to be enough, does it? Our hearts cry for something more.

Imagine we're Stradivarius violins, and no one nestled us under their chins or moved the bows to make our strings sing. I imagine my first question would be, "Am I important?"

And even if I were told, "Man, you're a *Stradivarius violin.* Of course you're important!" that wouldn't satisfy my question and the cry of my heart. I'd still want something more.

That reminds me of *Toy Story 2* when a toy collector named Al steals Woody and sells him as part of a collection of "Woody's Round-Up" dolls to a museum overseas. These toys are destined to be displayed in a glass case and preserved forever.

A great idea—at first. But Woody doesn't want to leave his loving owner, Andy. He wants to be what he was made to me: a toy, not a museum piece. Even though he's a valuable collectible, he wants something more. He wants love, and he's willing to give up his mint condition to get it.

Is it possible that we're really asking, "Am I valuable enough to be loved?"

Maybe that's what the obsession about appearance is all about. Maybe it isn't about makeup and magazines and photographs and muscles and haircuts and tans. Maybe it's about an obsession for love.

A LESSON LUCY LEARNED

In another story in C.S. Lewis' *The Voyage of the Dawn Treader,* the crew discovers on one particular island many invisible creatures that thump when they walk. These Thumpers surround the crew when they land ashore, and order them to send the girl (Lucy) to the scary Magician's house to read the spell to make hidden things visible.

It was an unfortunate turn of events, but there was nothing else to do. The Thumpers warn her that the Magician is a terrible man who "uglified" them and then turned them invisible. They say she may also meet her doom if he finds her prowling about.

So the following morning, Lucy creeps into the Magician's house to look for the spell book. Upstairs, she finds the library and the Magic Book sitting on a pedestal in the middle of the room. As she turns the pages, many different spells catch her attention. The first of which compels her to look at all the pictures that are coming to life on the page.

It was an "infallible spell to make beautiful her that uttereth it beyond the lot of mortals." In the pictures, Lucy sees a girl with a terrible expression on her face standing before a Magic Book and reciting a spell. Then she looks into the eyes of the girl in the picture, and she sees herself. The spell is already working on the Lucy in the picture, as the beauty beyond the lot of mortals comes to her. Then the pictures on the page all come to life.

Tournaments between kings and dukes who fight for Lucy's favor soon turn to wars, and all the lands of Narnia are laid waste because of Lucy's beauty. Then, once Lucy returns back to her own world, Lucy is even more beautiful than her older sister, Susan. Which means nobody cares about Susan anymore.

Lucy stands at the book, watching the pictures and deciding she will say the spell. But as soon as she looks back at the words of the spell, another picture appears large in the center of the page. It's a picture of a lion. Lucy knows that face well. It is Aslan, the King above all High Kings. He has an angry expression on his face, and he looks like he's growling. Lucy turns the page at once.

Have you ever wished you knew the words of that spell? I think we all have. Guys and girls alike all want attention like that. We believe love is found there.

Lucy finds many more spells in the book. She even recites some spells and sees terrible things happen. (You must read the book and find out what they are.) But then she finds the spell she's been looking for—the one that makes "hidden things visible."

First, she makes sure of the hard words, and then says it. She knows it's working because pictures start appearing on the pages. Now she suddenly realizes that many other invisible things may now be visible—things she'd never want to see.

But as she thinks this, some footsteps come up behind her. She remembers what the Thumpers said about what would happen if the Magician were to find her sneaking about. She turns around.

Then her face lit up till, for a moment (but of course she didn't know it), she looked almost as beautiful as that other Lucy in the picture, and she ran forward with a little cry of delight and with her arms stretched out. For what stood in the doorway was Aslan himself, The Lion, the highest of all High Kings. And he was solid and real and warm and he let her kiss him and bury herself in his shining mane. And from the low earthquake-like sound that came from inside him, Lucy even dared to think that he was purring.

Is it enough to believe we're made in God's image? I don't think so. We need something more. We need to know we're loved.

Growing up in church, I often heard we don't deserve God's love, that we're worthless like worms. And it puzzled me why God would love me if I were really worthless.

But I'm not a worm, and I'm not worthless. God made me valuable, even when I'm not living up to my potential all the time. God loved me enough to make me valuable, even before I was alive enough to know it.

And what does it mean to be loved by God? It means God has your best in mind for you. It means he draws near to you, has his eye on you, is pleased in you, and wants you to be his—part of his family, part of his kingdom. He has a free will and he has the ability to bring your good in this life and the next (if you'll let him).

I have a friend from the Czech Republic who is often caught walking around his apartment in the morning saying, "There is nothing I can do today to make God love me less."

Now that may be old to some, but it's new to others. And it's true. God does not love us because we act lovable all the time. God loves us because God wants to love us.[84] And God's love made us valuable in our very being, regardless of our merit. Period.

There is absolutely nothing bad that you can do to make God love you less. He loves you because you're an image bearer of him. God loves you because he made you. Add up all your bad things together, multiply them by a million, and know that God still loves you the same with his infinite love.

[84] 1 John 4:16, "And so we know and rely on the love God has for us. God is love. Whoever lives in love lives in God, and God in them."

Then my Czech friend will say, "There is nothing I can do to make God love me more." God is love. Period.

There is absolutely nothing good you can do to make God love you more. God loves you because you're an image bearer of him. God loves you because he made you. Add up all your good things together, multiply them by a million, and God still loves you the same with his white-hot infinite love.

Try to look like the folks in the magazines to find love—it doesn't matter. God doesn't love you any more than he already does. Try cutting yourself. God doesn't love you any less than he already does.

To do anything to make God love you more would be like painting your nails in the hope that it will earn you good grades, or inflating the tires on your car in the hope that it will give you a stylish haircut.

God is love, love, love, love, love.

God loves you down to the bone, down to the very center of your soul.

That is what we're looking for, after all. While the celebrities and models vie for the next cover of *Cosmo,* take a step back and remember who you are.

We don't have to be obsessed with our appearance anymore.

A NEW PERSPECTIVE

So what can we do about it? It's easy to talk about God loving us. And for many, that's all the perspective they need to explore those ideas and work them out in their lives.

Still others want to know what they can do to help climb out of the pit where they've been feeling so low about their value and their unloveliness. They want to know how to be free of the diversion.

No solution is easy because each of us struggles with our own sense of value for different reasons. (I struggle, in part, because of divorced parents.)

THE BEST ADVICE I CAN GIVE YOU IS TO UNPLUG YOURSELF. If you're into the opinions of the magazines, stop reading them for a while. Go without them for a week and see how it goes. Then try to go without them for two weeks. Then a month. Gauge yourself. Measure your desire for them and test your own motivations for clinging to them.

If you find yourself gravitating to pornography or "softer" forms of media that objectify women or men in sexy poses, unplug. If you find you don't have the strength to unplug, talk to a friend about it. (See www.xxxchurch.com for more ideas about unplugging.) Try to go without those glances for a week and see how it affects your tastes.

Part of living with questions is allowing ourselves to go through the discomfort that's required when we're trying to change certain aspects of our lives.

THE SECOND THING I WOULD SAY IS TO SPEND TIME THINKING ABOUT WHO TOLD YOU OR WHO STUNG YOU INTO THINKING YOU AREN'T LOVED OR VALUED. Identify those people, those names, those faces.

Then ask yourself whether they were telling the truth. If you really are made in God's image, then they didn't tell the truth. And you have to rethink the false belief you've held for so long. Then do your best to forgive those people. It's possible they are (and were) struggling with personal issues, too.

Maybe after you close the magazines and identify the source of your hurts, you can find some good literature about a woman's interior life, study some women in the Bible, or read the novels of L.M. Montgomery or the stories of Madeleine L'Engle or *Hannah Coulter* by Wendell Berry.

THE THIRD THING I WOULD SAY IS FIND PEOPLE WHO ARE CARING. This character trait may not exist among some of your friends—the ones you feel are always competing with you. Ask God to lead you to caring people so you have a safe place and safe relationships. Be prepared for God to bring along someone who's different from you, perhaps even someone who's quite a bit older or younger than you.

However, it won't happen if you're not proactive. And don't expect someone to come help you if they don't know you want their help.

THE FOURTH THING I WOULD DO IS ENCOURAGE YOU TO START PUTTING ON A NEW PERSPECTIVE ABOUT YOUR PURPOSE. Let's suppose something that many who are coping in the Wild would find crazy: *What if our appearance is what God intended? What if we look this way on purpose?*

What if God made us to look a certain way because that's our uniform as we go into Dragon-occupied territory? What if God made us a certain way because he knew that would be the look we needed in order to be effective image bearers of him? What if all our obsession about appearance, our extra hours spent in front of the mirror, our weekends spent at the mall, our worry over what others think about us—what if all of that actually got in the way of our mission?

It would be like Jack Bauer fretting over the color of his cell phone when he should be eavesdropping on the enemy's plans.

As I've said before, there's a great war between heaven and hell over whether God is good. And the battle is for our hearts.

What if our time spent playing dress-up actually puts us in the wrong place at the wrong time and with the wrong people? What if God doesn't want us to imitate models because he already has people in those places to shine his light? What if God wants us to be plain, ordinary, unobserved people who sprinkle peace and grace everywhere we go? Would you be all right with that?

Taking this new perspective, let's bundle up all our feelings of inadequacy, tie them up with a hard knot, and lay them at the feet of our Master Craftsman.

QUESTIONS TO LIVE INTO

What makes you feel most valuable?

What makes you feel least valuable?

What about your body do you dislike? Who told you it was unappealing? Why do you believe them?

Unplug. Put down the magazines or the online sites that objectify men and women. Try doing this for a week. Write down how you feel about it. Are your tastes changing?

How are you contributing to the false images in today's culture? How is your body manipulated to impress others by your stellar appearance?

Start a discussion group among peers to talk about how appearance affects you all. Call it "Renew" and make it a time to renew your minds with real ideas about men and women. Be intentional about noticing how advertisements change the way you view the opposite sex. Cut out advertisements and bring them to the group so you can analyze what the advertisements are saying. Draw up ways to deal with them and encourage each other. If you struggle with judging others by how their bodies look, check out Jonalyn Grace Fincher's book, *Ruby Slippers: How the Soul of a Woman Brings Her Home*, chapter 1.

How are you made in God's image? Be specific.

Write up a list of character qualities (not physical qualities) you're looking for in the opposite sex. How well do you live up to your own list?

Say this phrase every morning 10 times after you wake up: "I am a child and servant of the Most High God, my Father, who made me the way I am for a purpose."

Notes

_____

_____

_____

_____

_____

_____

_____

_____

QUESTION 6

AM I GOOD ENOUGH?

I stood in front of one painting longer than I stood in front of any other artwork in the entire exhibit.

On the left side of the canvas stands a woman in profile. Her shoulders slump slightly forward and her arm hangs down at her side. Her eyes are closed. She wears a white, cotton tank top, and her face is resolved, but cast in a shadow.

Standing behind her—also in profile but facing in the opposite direction—is the same woman. It's her mirror image. Only now her tank top is flattened in the front; where her breasts used to be are two large blood stains on her white shirt. With her eyes still closed, her face—filled more with resignation than anguish—is tilted up toward heaven. An inviting, soft light illuminates her face.[85]

[85] Melissa Weinman, St. Agatha's Grief, 1996. Oil on canvas, 42 x 42 in.

This work of art evokes my tears, as the woman's torment tugs at recent memories of my mother's breast cancer and resulting mastectomy.

The art exhibit was aptly named *A Broken Beauty*.[86]

The painting, called *St. Agatha's Grief*, captures the legend of Saint Agatha of Catania. As a young woman, Agatha committed herself to a life of chastity before God. When Agatha refused the advances of a powerful man in her village, he had her arrested and sent to live in a brothel for a month, hoping to tempt her to abandon her vow and her faith in God.

Unwilling to give up her commitment to God, Agatha was then brought before this powerful man who condemned her to be tortured and to have her breasts severed. It is said that while Agatha was bleeding in her cell, God sent to her a messenger with healing in his hands. He completely restored Agatha's breasts and filled her prison cell with light. When the powerful man discovered that Agatha had been healed, he ordered more torture and further imprisonment for her. So Agatha prayed and asked God to deliver her spirit to heaven—a prayer God painlessly and gracefully answered.[87]

The story of St. Agatha demonstrates that something is not right in this world. Not only was the powerful man twisted, but Agatha's body was also twisted and slashed.

Beauty, like many good things, is vulnerable to being twisted, defaced, and corrupted.

VALUABLE, BUT...

In the previous chapter, we discussed where our value lies.

But if I'm a valuable person, why don't I feel that way?

If God made me in his image and loves me, why does God feel so far away sometimes?

That's a question I've lived with for a long time.

When examining any belief system, whether old or new, it needs to explain what's wrong with the world in a way that satisfies our questions. Eastern religions will often say you need to negate all your desires or life is only an illusion or things need to be rebalanced.

---

[86] Visit the artists, ideas, and some of the artwork of A Broken Beauty at http://www.abrokenbeauty.com/.

[87] For one version of St. Agatha's story, go to http://www.catholic-forum.com/saints/sta04001.htm.

But those explanations invalidate the texture of my struggle and my question. These aren't just illusions. My desires are meaningful; they need to be explored, not denied. And I don't want a balance of good and evil, or a balance of healthiness and brokenness. I want goodness without evil. I want health without brokenness.

How does the Christian God answer this question: "Am I good enough?"

A BROKEN BEAUTY

It's obvious something isn't right with the world. We are troubled in the Wild.

Read the Google News headlines. Watch CNN. Read the stories in your own town's newspaper. Robberies, murders, tsunamis, blizzards, hurricanes, floods, backdated stock options, fraud, forgery, greed, homelessness, poverty, hunger, civil wars, terrorism, rape, forgery, and perjury.

On the street where I live, I've witnessed the S.W.A.T. team two times in the past year coming to rescue someone and arrest someone else. In my town, sirens race along the boulevard every day. Trees are cut down. Jobs are lost.

Hardship comes in spurts and waves. People cry and they laugh. Most dress up nicely, put on smiles, and ignore most of it, pretending everything is going all right.

"How are you doing?" is the common question.

"Good, fine, all right," is the usual reply.

But are we fine? We got up late. The shirt we wanted to wear wasn't clean. Our little sister hogged the bathroom when we needed to take a shower. We forgot our assignment for class. Our homework was so hard we felt stupid. We got a poor grade on our test. The rainy day cancels our after-school plans. We're still wondering if the guy or girl we're interested in likes us back (and they didn't look at us today the way they did yesterday, which really confuses and discourages us). Our friend posted something embarrassing about us on YouTube. Our parents scolded us for something they're worried about in our lives. And even the changes we *want* to make in our own lives seem harder to live up to once we start to make them.

We feel powerless over many things in our lives.

Then someone calls and asks, "How are you?" And we don't want to share the truth. And we probably *shouldn't* share the truth because the question wasn't intended to be an invitation for us to share. It's just a greeting. That's it.

But the question reminds us, almost daily, that things are not fine.

Because of the kind of work I do, people tell me things. And I hear stories that come from hidden hurts often masked behind popular fashions and pretty smiles. Ugly things. Pain. Depression. Stories about parents. Abandonment. Fear. Confusion. Resentment.

Life is difficult.

But it's weird how we seem to have this impression that life isn't supposed to be this hard or that we're not supposed to hit so many obstacles and experience so many heartaches along the way. It seems like we're made for better things.

We are image bearers of God, but we're also somewhat broken, afraid, hiding, and struggling.

My mom used to say that everyone has one or more of the following defects of character: fear, dishonesty, selfishness, and resentment. Then she'd ask me, "Which ones do you have?"

All of them rise off the page for me, each pointing to broken pieces in my soul, things I hide in the Wild and try to cover with diversions.

I have fears that tug at my insecurities and make me believe people don't really want to be my friends.

I slip into dishonesty and change the subject whenever the topic of conversation is about something I struggle with but don't want to admit to anyone.

I have selfishness that allows my interests and hobbies to override my desire to look out for the needs of those I love.

I have resentment that keeps brewing like a witch's caldron, even though I thought I had forgiven someone.

What has gone wrong?

THE BEGINNING

Genesis tells us a compelling story about brokenness. God creates the first humans, Adam and Eve, and gives them new opportunities. They get to be gardeners and zookeepers, protectors and overseers of the home they've been given. They are mini-creators, enjoying the pleasure of one another and having children.

Yet God also tells them to mind their own business. He says,

> *You are free to eat from any tree in the garden; but you must not eat from the tree of the knowledge of good and evil, for when you eat of it you will certainly die.* (Genesis 2:16-17)

You may ask, "Why did God put the tree there in the first place?"

I wonder the same thing. I have a hunch, though.

As an image bearer of God, we have a will. With a will comes the freedom to choose. For instance, when it's chilly outside, I can choose between a sweater and a coat. And when I'm thirsty, I can choose between milk and juice. Yet these are choices that have no moral connection. They're preferences, really. At face value, there is no right or wrong answer.

God has given us moral choices. *When the test is sitting on my desk, do I give my own answer or do I steal someone else's? When I find a wallet, do I return it to the owner with or without the cash inside? When you have dirt on someone, will you keep it to yourself or will you share it while issuing the "don't tell anyone" condition? (And then that person passes it on with the exact same condition.)*

The first humans had all sorts of daily choices to make. And among these was a moral choice.

Because Genesis is a narrative, it doesn't tell us the "whys" behind many things. We have to study it, think about it, compare it with the rest of the information we have about God, and make some deductions. (This is called "doing theology.")

So with moral choices comes a choice about love. Adam and Eve had to decide whether or not they believed God loved them. *Are they going to disbelieve God is all that smart or powerful or loving? Are they going to pretend they know more than God does? Will they take forbidden things into their own hands? Will they risk losing their Home?*

This is why God put the forbidden tree in the garden. It gave Adam and Eve an opportunity to really choose God's love.

So they walk about the garden, overseeing the animals and lying under the canopy of trees. They're near the forbidden tree—the Tree of the Knowledge of Good and Evil—when a snake walks up to Eve and starts talking to her, "Did God really say, 'You must not eat from any tree in the garden'?" (Genesis 3:1)

Do you notice his plan of attack? He nudges Eve to doubt what God said. He's not forcing her to eat the fruit outright. Instead, the serpent knows he must first drive a wedge of distrust between Eve and God. If Eve finds God suspicious, then she'll probably eat a piece of fruit from that tree.

Eve knows what God said, and she knows the consequences.

But the snake keeps talking.

"You will NOT die," the serpent said to the woman. "For God knows that when you eat of it your eyes will be opened, and you will be like God, knowing good and evil" (Genesis 3:4-5).

Basically, he's saying, "God doesn't want you to eat that fruit because it will benefit you. You'll be like God." He still hasn't tempted her to blatantly disobey God. He's just pushing her deeper into distrust. Deeper into thoughts of...

Is God concealing something?

Is God afraid I might become a challenge to him?

Did God make me incomplete?

Is God keeping something from me that's rightfully mine?

Eve looks at the fruit on that tree (Genesis doesn't tell us what kind of fruit it was), and she plucks a piece of it from a branch. It's smooth and beautiful, just like many things that don't belong to us. It doesn't *look* poisonous. She thinks it will make her wiser. And then she steals a bite of it. Adam is nearby, and he takes a bite, too.

In that moment, something suddenly shifts in the world, like a giant crack along a fault line in her soul.

Then man and woman become confused. They're frightened by their own vulnerable nakedness, so they sew some leaves together. And then they hide from God.

God calls for them. Out from the foliage emerge two humans with guilt on their faces, making excuses for why they hid from God.

God asks, "Who told you that you were naked? Have you eaten from the tree that I commanded you not to eat from?" (Genesis 3:11)

Adam quickly blames God and Eve, "The woman you put here with me—she gave me some fruit from the tree, and I ate it." (Genesis 3:12)

Eve diverts the pointed finger, "The serpent deceived me, and I ate."

THE RISE OF EVIL: TWISTED THINGS

Brokenness is what happens when evil has spun through our lives like a tornado. Adam and Eve found themselves kicked out of their Home and into the Wild. And they eventually died.

People today shy away from the word *evil* because it sounds judgmental. But we have to put aside our worries about judging others if we're going to find any kind of helpful answer to our question.

Evil has always been a parasite. It doesn't stand on its own two feet. It needs something good to ruin. Evil is not original, and it cannot make its own straight line, so it twists straight lines and makes them crooked.

Bananas are good, but they rot with age. That rot or decay is like evil. Decay wouldn't exist if something good, such as bananas, didn't exist in the first place.

Goodness creates life. Evil murders life.

Goodness creates gifts. Evil is the thievery that robs others of their gifts.

Goodness creates marriage. Evil twists it into divorce.

Goodness creates a beautiful face. Evil scars that face in an auto accident.

Think about Adam and Eve. Their life, their home, their food, and even the rules of the garden were all good. They stood up straight until evil cut them down. Evil took God's good things and twisted them.

Think about a serial killer. He was given the gift of life; but evil choices twisted his life and sent him off to wreck others' lives.

Or think about cancer. It preys on life and only dies when that life dies. Philosophers call disease, hurricanes, tsunamis, and volcanoes "natural evil." These are things that seem to have gone awry and hurt the good things we find, especially human life.

Throughout the Bible, evil is seen as a corruption of good things. Saint Augustine of Hippo more than 1,500 years ago stated it like this: "Evil is a privation of the good." In other words, evil needs good things to exist and to prey upon.

Goodness is the original life-giving thing. Evil is utterly unoriginal.

J.R.R. Tolkien understood this about evil. In the larger story of Middle-Earth, Dark Lords created evil creatures to mock the good creatures. Trolls were made to mock the Ents, and Orcs were made to mock the Elves.

And the Hobbits? What happens when they're twisted? Bilbo Baggins discovered a Hobbit who'd been twisted by evil, sitting alone in a dark cave. The pathetic creature had an appetite for raw meat, biting the flesh off of fish while he bartered for Bilbo's life through his riddles.

Poor Smeogol. Once a humble Hobbit, his lazy life was corrupted. His goodness was bent when he found the One Ring and possessed it as his own. The slow transformation began, and Smeogol became Gollum.

He possessed the One Ring, but then it slowly possessed him.

Like biochemical weapons, all evil needs to find open cracks in the doors of our souls. Then it takes up residence, possesses us, grows, and slowly poisons us.

EVIL MISSES THE MARK

The Bible uses an old word that has lost its meaning these days. This word is used for movie titles or even to joke about pleasure. I've seen items in restaurant menus described with this word: "This chocolate cake is simply *sinful*."

Sin is a word that literally means "to miss the mark." And when the chocolate cake you ordered "misses the mark" then you return it to the chef.

If your mechanic "misses the mark" when he's repairing your car, then you don't pay him.

If your doctor "misses the mark" when prescribing your medication, then you require her to try again and get it right.

If your computer "misses the mark" by incessantly crashing, then you order new parts for it.

Nobody wants things that miss the mark and don't work the way they should. We don't want broken things.

Yet this is the very thing that has happened to us. We "miss the mark" of being whole humans all the time.

And others put lies on us that only double our difficulty.

I mentioned earlier that I come from a broken home. My dad left us when I was six years old, and my sister and I occasionally visited him while we were growing up.

My mother was concerned about how we would grow up and the choices we would make. She knew the world and understood life in the Wild. There were far more opportunities for us to do evil than good.

One of her fears was that we would make some of the same choices our father did. Mom wanted something better for us, but her fear came out like this, "Don't end up like your father!"

She meant well; however, she didn't think through the meaning of her statement. In many ways I *would* be like my father. I am a Fincher, after all. I share the same gene pool. And certain gestures I'll make in the mirror, certain inflections of my voice, certain ways of reasoning—they all remind me of my father. And my father wasn't all that bad: I've learned many good things from him, too. And all these are things I cannot escape.

Yet I felt like running from the inescapable, and I even resented myself for not living up to my mother's advice, "Don't end up like your father!"

Before I married Jonalyn, I met with a Christian counselor for several months. This issue was one of the many things we discussed. When I finished sharing with the counselor the story I just shared with you, I added, "I just don't think I can escape it. The Bible does say that God punishes 'the children for the sin of the fathers to the third and fourth generation…'" I knew the punishment came from following in the sin of our parents. I wanted to be so free from bad choices, but I was afraid I was stuck being like my father, without hope or help to be myself.

Then my counselor said to me, "Finish the verse." My mind went blank. She continued, "Showing love to a thousand generations of those who love me and keep my commandments."[88]

I knew the rest of that verse, but for some reason it never occurred to me to apply it to this situation.

"Do you love God?" she asked. I nodded. "Then you don't have to worry."

She shared with me that what my mother had done was give me a "curse." She put a false belief on my head that was virtually inescapable. And I'd carried the burden without question.

I was light on my feet when I left the counselor's office that day. I felt as though the brokenness I'd experienced under that curse was healed. I loved God and that was enough.

Later that week I called my mother and explained my experience. She apologized for putting that kind of burden on me, even though it was well intended. We drew closer because of it.

This false belief about me wasn't the only curse I carried. I still have many others, most of which I'm still unaware.

It's likely that you also carry curses that add an extra weight onto your shoulders. Perhaps you come from a family who blames and shames you in order to motivate you to do what they want. Maybe some have called you names, throwing them like daggers, and you've slowly learned to believe these labels are really true. Maybe you believe you're unimportant or

---

[88] Exodus 20:4-6.

not good enough because curses are lodged in your soul, and you haven't
identified them yet.

Missing the mark is failing to live up to our title as image bearers of
God. It's bad enough when we know we're broken. It adds to the burden when others heap curses and burdens on us that only deepen our
wounds.

EVIL MURDERS LOVE

A word picture of sin I appreciate for its frankness is this: Sin is lifting
your middle finger to God and saying, "Buzz off!"

I believe that's the overarching idea of sin in the whole Bible. Sin isn't
merely a matter of "disobeying" or "doing something wrong" or "breaking the law." Sin is missing the mark foremost by breaking relationships.

In the Old Testament, God gives the Israelites laws on how to conduct
their society as image bearers of him. People often refer to these as the
Ten Commandments (Exodus 20). But the book of Deuteronomy adds
a few more to the list—more than 600! God gave his people these laws
because they were living in the Wild, and they didn't naturally do what
was right and just.

When we run about and try our best to discover what is right and
wrong, it can often be confusing. So many voices offer us different opinions. However, the Israelites didn't view God's laws as arbitrary dos and
don'ts that God created just to make them miserable. They were intended, in part, to create order for their society. They were also intended, in
part, to let the Israelites know what the character of God is like. The law
was a signpost for free travelers. People were supposed to check out the
Israelites and get a picture of God.

After God rescues the Israelites from slavery in Egypt, he leads them
to a mountain called Sinai. They'd seen what God is like in terms of
power and deliverance when they crossed the Red Sea. But at Mount
Sinai they see God's heart. They see God's character. They see what kind
of souls they were created to have—large souls, ordered and free.

That's the spirit behind the Law of God. And this spirit is summarized
in just a few short words at the beginning of Deuteronomy. Jesus quotes
it in this scene from Matthew 22:34-40.

The Pharisees, strict keepers of the Law, approach Jesus to test him with some questions. They often did this, trying to trip him up and hurt his credibility. So, one of their top experts presents a tough question. This man doesn't live with questions the way you and I do. He likes to spin trick questions just to fluster people.

He asks Jesus, "Teacher, which is the greatest commandment in the Law?"

If someone were to ask you this question about our country's laws, what would you say? I'm not sure what I would say. Right to a trial? Freedom of religion? Writ of Habeaus Corpus? Freedom of speech? The right to vote? Freedom to own property? Freedom to pursue happiness? Maybe just "freedom"? But people don't often think of "freedom" as a law, although laws protect freedom.

Jesus has the answer on the tip of his tongue. And we know the answer is good because Matthew writes in verse 46, "from that day on no one dared to ask him any more questions."

Jesus answered:

'Love the Lord your God with all your heart and with all your soul and with all your mind.' This is the first and greatest commandment. And the second is like it: 'Love your neighbor as yourself.' All the Law and the Prophets hang on these two commandments. (Matthew 22:37-40)

When an ancient Jew used the phrase "All the Law and the Prophets," that was a quick way to say, "all the Scriptures," for the Old Testament is largely made up of writings of the law and the prophets' written history of Israel.

So Jesus was saying that all the laws have to do with love—loving God and loving others. And when love happens, it brings freedom, wholeness, healing.

When I think back to the Garden of Eden, I can see that Adam and Eve didn't break an arbitrary law. They betrayed their friendship with God.

Adam and Even chose to lift their middle fingers to God. And when we sin, it twists not only our souls, but also our connection with God and our friendships with each other. Every time you do something to damage a relationship with someone, it's sin. And every time you do something to create or mend a relationship, it's love.

SIN'S CALCULATION

Sin calculates how far it will knock you off your feet. The more you know what's right, the harder you'll fall for rejecting it. Jesus didn't speak the most harshly to the woman caught in adultery but to the Pharisees and teachers of the law who were ready to stone her to death. They knew better and had better opportunities, yet they still chose evil.

Leaders fall hard. And religious leaders fall harder still. But the one who's fallen hardest of all is Lucifer, the Dragon, because he once stood in the presence of God.[89]

That's the danger of sin in the Wild. The more we understand the Wild and how to journey Home, the worse our souls grow if we ignore it. That's why it's immoral to reject truth when it's presented to you. It may actually leave you worse than the way it found you. Not because it's malicious, but because you have to close off part of your soul to reject it. You calcify your heart when you deny the life of goodness.

THE OPPOSITES

Sin and love are opposites. Sin will shape us into things we're not meant to be. It will make us mean, greedy, lustful, proud, distrustful, isolated, deceitful, or ashamed. It will make us into a twisted human, like the way Gollum was a twisted hobbit.

Love, on the other hand, will bring life, encouragement, a clear head for romance, appropriate acts of justice, friendship, attractive vulnerability, freedom, and kindness. It will make us into a whole human, free, like the way Gandalf and Galadriel were whole and free.

No wonder the Bible uses a word like *righteousness*. It essentially means to be what you were made to be—designed to have God's character. You and I are to be righteous. We are to love the *right* way.

This is quite different than our misconceptions of do's and don'ts and the

---

[89] This is an old idea found in C.S. Lewis, *Reflections on the Psalms*.

many regulations we feel God puts on us for no good reason at all. Maybe we should pause to think about what God's real reasons are. And, even more, maybe we should pause and figure out why rules bother us so much.

THE BROKENNESS WITHIN

We are broken because we are victims of others. But we are also broken because we are victims of our own poor choices and our inability to do things right. We have a divide between knowing what love is and actually being loving toward others. And that divide should be a terrible concern to us.

One of the people who became a devout follower of Jesus and ended up writing more of the New Testament than any other individual was named Paul.

Paul was a Pharisee and an incredible intellectual. He also persecuted Christians early in his career. Then Jesus met him on the road to Damascus and changed his life.

Paul understood the law as well as any of the experts. He also understood himself and knew how broken he was.

That's why he penned in his letter to the believers in Rome, "For all have sinned and fall short of the glory of God" (Romans 3:23).

In other words, we're all broken, and we don't have direct access to a friendship with God because of it. We're like the rotten banana that's no longer good for eating. We're like the broken computer that isn't fit for the office. We just aren't fit for God's family and God's kingdom.

We don't have to point fingers at everyone else and ask, "Do they have sin? Are they broken?" We just need to ask ourselves. This is about us. We know if we have sin. We know if we're broken.

Once we admit that, then our next and more difficult question is, *Who will deliver me, mend me, rescue me, help me, and love me back to being what I'm supposed to be?*

Our Deliverer cannot be someone who's living in the Wild with us. For we in the Wild can only huddle together; we cannot find our way out. Only someone outside of the Wild can guide us. We need someone with a bird's eye view. We need someone who knows the way Home and can lead us there. We need someone who remembers the songs of Eden and can sing them to us again.

Nevertheless, we often try to help ourselves. There are plenty of books and television shows that try to point the way. I once watched an episode of *Oprah* during which she interviewed a guest who'd gone through a lot of stress due to abuse and a bad family life. As Oprah ended her show, she looked into the camera and said, "What we've learned today is that the greatest love of all is the love of self."

I almost fell out of my chair. It was the last answer I would expect to hear. I do love myself, but my love is feeble and inward. I need someone who's bigger than me to love me. I need Someone who will draw me outward.

I know many people gravitate to self-help. This is about the best they can do if they're confused in the Wild and not searching for God.

And that's another reason I find Christianity to be true. It offers Someone from the outside who stepped into the Wild, drew close enough for me to hear and know him, yet still has the power to lead me Homeward.

This is what Jesus was all about.

The Israelites heard about the promised Messiah for centuries. And one day he showed up, born of a virgin girl.

Messiah means "Chosen One." The prophet Isaiah anticipated his coming. He called the Messiah "Wonderful Counselor, Mighty God, Everlasting Father, Prince of Peace" (Isaiah 9:6). And when the Messiah shows up, he's received by some as the Lord's salvation (Luke 2:28-32).

"Joshua" would be the Savior's name if we translated it straight from Hebrew. But we use the Greek form of his name: Jesus.

Among the titles Jesus used for himself, the one he used most often was "Son of Man." This was not a lowly term. This was like saying, "Of all the men who have ever lived, I am THE man." Perhaps it was even a claim of deity. He identified himself as the Son of mankind, the one who would represent all of us.

Paul later said that Jesus was the "last Adam" (1 Corinthians 15:45). And with those words, it all becomes clear what Jesus came to do.

The first Adam sent us into the Wild, and we've been living with our own evil and brokenness ever since. The last Adam came to lead us back and make us fit for Home.

You've seen the most popular symbol in Christianity: the cross. It's not just a good-luck charm. And it's not a symbol to make us feel more spiritual. The cross is an ancient form of execution upon which Jesus died at the hands of wicked people.

Jesus was tortured. He wore thorny brambles that penetrated his scalp. His hands and feet were pierced with large spikes. And he hung on cross-shaped beams, left to either suffocate or bleed to death, whichever came first.

As Jesus hung there, he looked down at those who were killing him and said, "Father, forgive them, for they do not know what they are doing" (Luke 23:34). What kind of love is this? What kind of Man is this who has a God's eye view of humans in the Wild, yet he can look with pity upon those who are destroying his body and still speak of forgiveness?

His last words were, "It is finished" (John 19:30).

What was finished? What does this all mean? It means Jesus took all of the evil of the world—including ours—upon his own shoulders. His spilled blood is like medicine for our corruption. He came to mend us of all the scars of brokenness and death.

And we know it worked because Jesus did something no other person in history has ever experienced. He came back to life again. We looked at some historical evidence for this in the fourth chapter, "Question 4—Has God Spoken?" But that it happened isn't enough for us. We must realize the significance of his resurrection; this dying and rising God is who we need most.

Paul writes, "God made him who had no sin to be sin for us, so that in him we might become the righteousness of God" (2 Corinthians 5:21).

Do you see what he's saying? We can become righteous. We can do and love the right kind of way. We can begin our journey out of the Wild.

But there's something more going on here. Not only has our Deliverer come to mend our brokenness, but he also came to heal a relationship.

Jesus came to reconcile us with God. We told him to "buzz off!" Yet we don't have to be that way anymore. Although we offended God, through Jesus we are forgiven by God, and we are invited to be his kids.

Only then can we know the Prince of Peace. Peace is not an absence of conflict. Peace is when everything is just and right. And only Jesus can offer that.

HOW TO MEND

Isn't this what we've been looking for? Haven't we been looking for mending and healing all along? Haven't we wondered who will help us love others so we can get out of the soap-opera life some of us have been living? Haven't we grown weary with how difficult it is to change the things in our lives that we don't like?

Now we have the information. We're broken and a Healer has come. So what are we going to do about it?

I talked about faith in first two chapters, and this is where faith really happens. Faith is trusting God. It's identifying with Jesus and allowing his righteousness to be your new clothing. It's trusting God's forgiveness.

When you choose to be God's friend through Jesus, you may not have any special feelings. It's merely a choice to receive life.

And how will you know God has heard you? Well, do you believe God would do so much as to send himself to deliver you from the Wild and then allow your prayer for deliverance to go unheard? Absolutely not. When you choose to follow God, you become his friend. It's the beginning of deliverance.

But it isn't merely about being forgiven. It's about being made new. Jesus calls this a new birth (John 3:3-8). I like that imagery. We were fresh and new when we were born from our mothers; now we are new again, spiritually born from God. It's a completely fresh start. It's walking into the new life God has offered you—to walk in God's love and be appropriately human.

He will empower us to grow to love the way he loves. As Ravi Zacharias has noted, Jesus will not only change what we do, he will also change what we want to do.

We're no longer enemies of God or strangers to God. We become like Abraham—God's friend. And even more, we become a son or daughter of the Most High King.

Am I good enough? I'm afraid not.

But there's Someone who is. Someone who will clean us up, bandage our souls, smooth out the twisting sin does to us, and put us back on our feet. This Someone doesn't come from within the Wild, but from outside of it. He invaded history to rescue us, and now he invites us to follow him Home.

QUESTIONS TO LIVE INTO

How are you broken? Where do you see unhealthiness in your life?

Which defects of character do you struggle with: Fear, dishonesty, selfishness, resentment?

How are you like Adam and Eve, convinced that God is not really trustworthy? In what areas do you not trust God?

Have you caught yourself wondering, as Eve may have:
    Is God concealing something?

Did God make me incomplete?

Is God keeping something from me that's rightfully mine?

What does it mean that evil is a parasite? Have you seen evil corrupt something good in your life?

In the story about my mom, I talk about a "curse" or a lie that was put on me. Who has put curses on you? Can you identify a label or an insult that you remember from a while ago that still rattles around in your mind, hurting you and keeping you from being a free image bearer of God? What is it?

Do you feel like Christianity is a big list of dos and don'ts? If so, why?

Do you agree with this statement? "Every time you do something to damage a relationship with someone, it's sin. And every time you do something to create or mend a relationship, it's love."

If so, what do you need to do to spread more love?

Think about the one sin that keeps tripping you up. Then write a response to this question: "If I can trust Jesus with all of eternity, why can't I trust him to help me change now?"

What does it mean to become more "appropriately human"? Visit www.soulation.org and look up some articles in "The Library." Try to understand what it means to be a whole human.

Notes

_____

_____

_____

_____

_____

_____

_____

_____

_____

_____

_____

_____

LIVING WITH QUESTIONS

QUESTION 7

WHAT'S SO GREAT ABOUT HEAVEN?

The statistic for death on planet Earth has been carefully researched. So far the numbers stand at 100 percent.

Or as William Wallace's father memorably said to him in *Braveheart*, "All men die. Not all men really live."

ALL PEOPLE DIE

We are mortals, but only in the sense that our bodies cannot endure forever. God told us this was part of our curse for betraying him: "For dust you are, and to dust you will return" (Genesis 3:19).

Sit for a moment and think about your temporariness. Death is always creeping in.

SUDDEN DEATH

When I was in college, I received a phone call that told me a friend of mine had died on his motorcycle. I was dizzy and quiet and felt strangely alone.

In 1997, I remember the month in which the world lost three key figures:

Princess Diana died—a shock well described in the movie *The Queen*.

Mother Teresa died—the caretaker of the needy in Calcutta, India. Her reputation of virtue has been heralded as one of the greatest in modern times.

Rich Mullins died—one of the few songwriters in the Christian music industry to honestly speak of our human condition in poetry that colored all of life. I didn't think of him as a "Christian singer." I thought of him as a human singer who understood the meaning of things.

The first two deaths rocked the world. The last one rocked *my* world. When Rich Mullins died, I lost someone who helped me see God more clearly than almost anyone else. Rich sang the songs of Home when I was staggering in the dark of the Wild. I met him several times, waiting in the crowds of people to get his autograph, listening to his words, and having a few brief conversations. Today, I still want to hear his songs that will never be written.

These deaths were tragic. They were tragic because they were sudden. And tragedy hits us like a punch in the chest.

But gradual deaths are tragic, too.

GRADUAL DEATH

When I was in college, my mom usually called me at random times. After dinner one Fall evening, I was alone in my dorm room, going through some reading for class. The phone rang.

This time she shocked me with her news. She told me her recent doctor's appointment had revealed a lump in her breast. They needed to do a biopsy to see if it was cancerous.

I listened. Coming from a non-emotional family, we stated things frankly. We could brave the strongest winds without collapsing into un-controllable crying.

As I listened to my mom talk, her news didn't feel like a punch in the chest. In fact, we didn't know what the lump was. But it did feel like a slow wringing of my soul.

Slowly, I responded as she spoke. *Yes. Okay. Uh-huh. When is the appointment?* But I couldn't hold onto what I was feeling. From deep down, the weight of the future pushed its way into my eyes. I began to wipe away tears. My matter-of-factness and the strength of my voice on the phone began to quiver. I was afraid. *What if the biopsy revealed cancer? Would there be hope for recovery? Would my mom suffer? What would I do? What would we do as a family? What does it mean?*

Two weeks later my mother went in for surgery. She told the doctor that if the lump was cancerous, they should remove her breast during the surgery.

When she awoke, one breast was gone.

It's tragic to discover you have a terminal disease. And while your death may not be sudden, it will come. Your days are numbered.

But isn't it just as tragic that death happens at all? We all have a terminal disease of some sort. It's not just that we'll all die some day. We're all dying *now*. Our bodies are decaying. We're older now than we were yesterday, more vulnerable to disease. And we'll be even older again tomorrow. The older we get, the more quickly time seems to pass. Our death day approaches.

I look at my hands and notice the creases getting deeper and the scars growing more numerous. My library of memories grows because I've spent more time on the earth in which to gather more memories.

One day you and I will be dead.

I'm not trying to be morbid. I'm trying to pay attention to a real part of life that's usually just tucked away in hospitals and mortuaries. We're afraid of death. So afraid, we don't talk about it. It confronts us with questions of how we're living life and preparing for death.

One man observed that we're as afraid today to talk about death as Victorians were afraid to talk about sex.[90] We're prudes when it comes to death. Victoria's little secret is now well known. When will we get honest about our own little secret—our fear of death?

GETTING HONEST

Some students are honest about their fear of death and their expectations of the afterlife. And their honesty sometimes reveals widespread misconceptions. Still, I respect their bravery to at least voice their questions. Because they're searching they'll be the first ones to figure out an answer.

As I thumb through a stack of 3 x 5 cards from students, various questions stand out:

Is it boring in heaven? How can we have fun in one place forever?

This is a student who apparently enjoys travel. But he's also assuming heaven is either small or like an island or maybe downtown Manhattan, where no matter which way you look, you're boxed in by skyscrapers. I want to reply, "What do you mean by 'place'?" The universe is a "place,"

[90] Joseph Bayly, *The Last Thing We Talk About.*

and it's plenty big. And I wouldn't be surprised if we eventually find heaven even bigger.

How does your soul go to heaven if you aren't really alive?

This student is unsure about a couple things. First—what it means to be alive or dead. She assumes that if you're body is dead, then all of you is dead. But that's not how the Bible views death. Death is a separation. You don't go unconscious when you die. Instead, your soul separates from your body. But *you* (your soul) are still alive.[91]

The second thing is her soul. She holds a popular assumption that her soul is just a part of her, like a finger-nail that you can easily cut off when it gets too long. She doesn't realize that her soul *is* her, that *she* is the one going to another place.

There's an old saying that helps explain the difference well; it goes like this, *I am a soul; I have a body.*

When I say, "I enjoy ice cream," I'm referring to someone who is enjoying the ice cream. Who is the "I"? It's me—Dale. But where am I in my body? It seems odd to say I'm in my toe or my knee. I don't experience life as a knee. When people have a leg or arm amputated, they still exist. So I'm not in my appendages.

Could I be in my brain? Perhaps. But then how do you explain those who've had half of their brains removed because of Rasmussen syndrome? Would we say they're now half people? They're still whole people, but with half of their brains.

So where am I? I'm a soul. I cannot be found in my body. I can be manipulated within my body by poking things in my brain. You can prick my finger and I will feel pain. But I'm not my brain, and I'm not my finger. I am a soul.

THE GOD INVASION

Isn't it bizarre to realize life won't go on like this forever? When I remember that one day life as I know it will end, I have this natural response that there's something after death. I wonder how we came to be lost in the

---

[91] 2 Corinthians 5:1-10; Philippians 1:20-26.

Wild, what we're supposed to do with it, and how we're supposed to find our way Home. This is where God's supposed to come in, right?

What's with the God invasion?

I received a collection of e-mails from a student who is sincerely troubled by why she exists. She wonders why God would create people and allow them to exist, but then tell them they must either believe in him or suffer in the afterlife. She believes God is unjust to create humans whom he knows will live an eternally suffering existence.

It's a troubling question to wrestle with and live with.

My suspicion is that she, like many today, assumes the story of our planet begins with *us*. I believe she also assumes we're just minding our own business in the cosmos, hiding in some corner and getting high on diversion, when suddenly some god on his morning stroll through the universe catches a glimpse of our planet and comes in for a closer look.

He likes this little orb of blue. He feels insecure about himself and decides he wants these little people to like him. It will make him feel better if they worship him, so he appears to a few; he even gives them laws to live by that he magically writes on a stone tablet. Since this god is powerful enough to cage our souls—even if we die—he can coerce us into bowing down before him. If we don't, he threatens to torture us after we die. And if we're unlucky, he might start torturing us *before* we die.

So, in effect, there is no real freedom to choose this god. You simply pretend you love him by reciting certain beliefs or praying certain prayers so you don't have to suffer his torments.

A lot of people assume this kind of story when they consider God, heaven, and hell. To them, God is a third party who stands on the outside and has always been on the outside. God intrudes into our daily lives and wants us to pay attention to him. God is selfish and demanding and even rude. We don't think God has any right to ask us to worship him. We don't believe God really knows what we need.

But that's the weird thing about it. God didn't just discover this world one day while he was strolling through the galaxy. God isn't pushing himself on us.

Saint Augustine reverses our perspective around in the opening of his *Confessions:*

You have made us for yourself. And our hearts are restless until they rest in you.

In other words, God made us. He didn't *discover* us, and we aren't minding our own business. Our primary business is God. There may be nothing better for us to do than to mind the business of God and get to know him.

God has made us for himself.

GOD KNOWS OUR NEEDS

And if God is as good as all indications say he is, then God knows our needs.

Imagine your wanting the best for someone or something. What if you had a new puppy? Would you simply leave the puppy to use its crate as a bathroom and whine for food? Would you let the dog nibble on a dead rat in the backyard while you had some juicy, meaty dog food for him inside the house?

It would only make sense to give the best to the puppy. That's what good owners do.

What if the puppy felt threatened when you said to him, "Eating that dead rat will make you sick!" What if he stuck up his head and replied, "You're not a good owner. You should leave me to my own business."

We are not God's pets. But some of this analogy really fits our situation. If God is the maker and owner of this world, which includes us, God knows when we're doing something that hurts us. God knows if we can live better lives. God knows the best way to be human, the best way to enjoy reality.

What is the best we could have in God's wide world?

Many times we nibble on lesser foods for our souls—diversions we find in the Wild, such as feeding on a friend's approval, moping in a puddle of self-consciousness, running after desires for things we know aren't good for us, licking our own proverbial dead rats—when God is offering us real food.

Our souls' food is God himself. We were made to run on the life of God. This is the Bread of Life.[92]

You see, walking away from God is just walking into nowhere. There is no such thing as "minding our own business." Either we can walk the trail or we can walk off the cliff. That's all there is. Some people believe God should make another place, a place where they can enjoy life without having God distracting them. If God could, he possibly would. But since God *is* the life (Jesus said, "I am the life"), he can't give you a good life without giving you himself. The good life is inseparable from God.

All these assumptions about God forcing himself on people just don't work with what we know. You either get God and joy and goodness—or you don't.

Knowing God is the natural thing. It's rejecting God that's unnatural.

THE PROBLEM OF HELL

If all this is true about God and us, which I believe it is, then hell becomes an important point.

Hell would then mean "to be cut off from God and life and goodness." The idea that there's partying in hell doesn't make any sense. For even partying carries full moments of joy and goodness, and those feelings have their source in God. Hanging out with your friends won't happen in hell because there is joy and goodness in that, and those feelings are only found with God.

You see, the things we really enjoy about life are all things that first find their place in God—

[92] John 6:35.

love

                    peace

        music

                  pleasure

   joy

           happiness

                            friends

       family

                     celebrations

              free time

        imagination

     leisure

                         fulfilling work

          smiles

                  good stories

    health

        intimacy

                       safety

            victory

      hope

        art

                     kindness

           strength

   creativity

If we don't understand this, we've completely misunderstood who God is. And we aren't rejecting *God* but a caricature we've made of him.

I get many questions about why God would send people to hell. And I understand the question and wrestle with it myself.

Then I think about society and wonder why these same people have less of a problem with judges sending people to prison for life. I believe people have a problem with hell because they assume it's too long or too hot or too final. "Someone wouldn't deserve a punishment like hell! Few people are that guilty!" goes the reasoning.

I don't look at hell like that. I don't believe God "sends" people to hell. I think it's just the opposite. God is fair enough that, if we don't want him, then we don't have to have him. We send ourselves to hell. Hell is a place that has a dead-bolt on the inside. Hell is the culmination of being our own god, the way Adam and Eve ate the fruit in the garden so they could be "like God."[93] Hell is Frank Sinatra singing, "I did it my way!" Hell is a place God has created so you can be as separated from him as possible.

This is part of living with the question of heaven and hell. They aren't destinations for those who've done a certain number of good or bad things. They are places for those who receive or reject the great Fountain of Love.

Think about it. Wouldn't it be wicked of God to demand that those who don't like him spend forever with him?

If we went to Paradise without receiving God's love, Paradise would be a version of hell for us. Forced to stand by a pure goodness we hate is not Paradise. Take all the palm trees, jewels, and streets of gold—even if you're surrounded by all of these beautiful things, nothing about Paradise would negate the fact that you're stuck in your Enemy's house.

In the Christian story, you either know the love you were designed to know and revel in the joy that's designed to fill you up—or you don't. One is love as you've always dreamed. The other is rejection as you've always feared. In the Christian story, love is called heaven and rejection is called hell.

The problem of hell, then, isn't a God problem; it's a problem with anyone who would choose to be there. I'm often surprised that when talking with some people, the more heated they get about the Bible, the more they reveal that it isn't a lack of understanding that frustrates them; it's anger that God is asking them to be loved. Some believe there's just too much personal risk to be loved by God.

HEAVEN

It might be helpful to think of heaven and hell as beginning in this earthly life. Either we love God in this life or we don't. Either we have spiritual separation from God in this life or we don't.

[93] Genesis 3:4, 5.

ETERNAL LIFE

Jesus made a remark about this when talking to a religious leader named Nicodemus (John 3:1-21).

Nicodemus is part of the religious elite in his community. Because he's afraid to live with questions in the daylight (where others might reject him), he sneaks out one night to find Jesus. He wants to know who Jesus really is and where he came from.

Jesus replies without directly answering Nicodemus's questions, "Very truly I tell you, no one can see the kingdom of God without being born again" (John 3:3).

Such a peculiar reply. Yet Nicodemus doesn't wrinkle his brow over it. He just follows up with the next question:

"How can anyone be born when they are old?" (John 3:4)

Jesus goes on to explain that he must be born of the Spirit. Being born of the Spirit is the beginning of heaven.

Nicodemus goes back and forth with Jesus, asking more questions until Jesus finally spells it out plainly. If we didn't have Nicodemus living with his questions, then we wouldn't have John 3:16:

For God so loved the world that he gave his one and only Son, that whoever believes in him shall not perish but have eternal life.

It's a powerful promise and opportunity. Yet the rest of Jesus' paragraph is usually missed.

For God did not send his Son into the world to condemn the world, but to save the world through him. Whoever believes in him is not condemned, but whoever does not believe stands condemned already because they have not believed in the name of God's one and only Son. (John 3:17-18)

When you look at the passage in context, it's clear that Jesus has an insight into heaven and hell, life and death. That's important for us to know. When Jesus says, "Whoever does not believe stands condemned already," he is talking about the present tense. Either you're feeding on

God's love and life now—or you're not. It isn't about what happens after our souls leave behind our bodies on our deathbeds. It's about what's going on *right now.*

You see, Jesus is telling us something special about "eternal life." He isn't say it's a life that begins after we die. Our souls are already lost until we find eternal life. Eternal life begins the day we turn to God.

CLOCK TIME

Eternal life isn't merely about clock time. Jesus isn't saying, "If you believe in God, you'll have many more hours tacked onto your life." Living longer is only a good thing if your life is good. Finding the foundation of youth isn't at the heart of what Jesus is saying.

ETERNAL QUALITY

Jesus speaks of eternal life as a new kind of quality. What do I mean by "quality"? I mean it in the sense of going from fool's gold to real gold. It's the quality of going from driving a Kia to driving a Ferrari. It's the quality of going from having no medicine to having lots of medicine. It's the quality of going from a weed to an orchid. Or the quality of meaninglessness to as much meaning as you can handle.

I'm not saying eternal life gives you gold and nice cars and good health in this life. Most of us may never see these things. But each of these things is a picture of good quality, and this is what Jesus wants for us—not quality of stuff, but quality of life.

But Jesus is saying our souls will go from wasting our lives on false gods to embracing the living God. Our souls will no longer stagger around in the Wild, but will find the freedom to choose well and relish goodness. Our souls will no longer get trapped in the dungeons of guilt but will move toward others, giving and receiving love. Our souls will no longer choke and cough on illegitimate pleasures that kill, but will drink joy from the Fountain of Joy.

Our souls will find peace, even if we're poor or ill. And our souls will know their purpose, even when they sit in suffering.

This is the eternal life that begins in *this* life. This is how heaven comes near. This is how the light shines in to clean out all the corrosions of our own selfishness, fears, dishonesties, and resentments.

And this kind of life, this free life, is what goes on and on and on.

DEATH LOSES

Death then loses its punch.[94]

Oh, we may still fear death. I know I do. I don't want to die. I fear how I will die. *What pain will I be in? What will those first moments after death be like? Will the things I believe be the way things really are?*

But we won't have to fear separation, emptiness, or being cut off from love.

And death itself, for those who love God, is no longer a striking down but a setting free.

I was at my mother's bedside when she died of cancer. She was in her bedroom—the same one I would sneak into when I was a boy because everything felt safer in her room. After battling cancer for nine years, she was now surrounded by family as her breathing diminished. We held her arms and feet. I was standing at the foot her bed, holding onto her when her last breath gave way.

With all my heart, I said aloud through my tears, "Fly, Mom, fly." I looked up toward the ceiling and repeated the words, expecting to catch the last glimpse of her soul as she soared to her God.

For my mom, death was a setting free.

God told Adam and Eve in the Garden of Eden that if they ate of the tree, they would die. And die they did. They physically died. Their relationship with God also died in some sense. A divide came between them and God because of their own rebellion.

God said they would be cursed with many things, including returning to the dust. Their bodies would disintegrate. One day they would no longer continue on the earth.

---

[94] 1 Corinthains 15:55-57.

But in Jesus Christ, the deathblow is turned upside down. Instead of a severe judgment, death becomes a severe mercy. Death is the process we go through to shed off this carcass of a body. It's necessary to rid ourselves of so many wrong habits that are within our bodies. Discarding our decaying bodies helps us do that.

Because of the power of the death and resurrection of Jesus, death becomes something that leads to healing. Just as Jesus said, "Because I live, you also will live."[95]

RESURRECTION

Resurrection means to rise from the dead, not zombie-like, but full and whole.

When Jesus resurrected, he wasn't a spirit floating around and haunting Jerusalem. He was flesh and bone. The disciples touched him. Thomas put his fingers into the scarred holes in Jesus' hands. The disciples met Jesus on the seashore, and they even ate food with him.

His was a new body—the first time a new body had ever been given to a human being after the old body had died.

Three months before my mother died, she visited us in California. My memories of those final months are priceless, but nothing burns in my memory as vividly as a simple conversation we had at the breakfast table one morning.

Mom had undergone almost a dozen major chemotherapies throughout her nine-year battle with cancer. Some of them took her to the edge of life itself. Each of them wore her down, no matter how hard she fought.

As she weakened, the doctors couldn't give her the higher doses of chemo that were available because her body couldn't handle the poison. She was running out of options.

I said to her, "So, Mom, with all of these doctors and medicines, where is the hope?"

I expected her to say that new breakthroughs are offering her some new drugs to fight the cancer. I expected her to shed light on her medical situation. But she didn't say these things.

---

[95] John 14:19.

"The hope?" she said in her matter-of-fact way. "Son, the hope is in the resurrection."

That is the most profound answer we have in the Wild. How else do we do battle against the foe of death? How are we to be remade as human again?

My mother was right. If our bodies are to be remade, then they have to be resurrected. No chemicals can make this happen. Nothing can stop the decay. We need the severe mercy of death so we can be remade.

Only Jesus Christ offers a solid remedy, conquers the problem of evil and death, and invites us into it.

Jesus said, "I am the resurrection and the life."[96]

For though we will die, we will be alive again.

Just as Jesus bodily rose from the dead, those who love Jesus will also bodily rise. We who love the Fountain of Life will be given life in a new body.

OUR NEW HOME

But let me explain something. Heaven is a wonderful place. Jesus spoke of his Father's house and how he was preparing a place for us (John 14). But in heaven, we will still not have our new bodies. We will only be waiting for the right time to receive them. Heaven is not the end of the story. There is more.

Have you ever wondered why you have the feeling you're not supposed to die? Well, I don't believe we were created to die and live in merely an immaterial place forever. I believe God intended us to be earth dwellers forever. And earth dwellers we will remain.

This is a different viewpoint than many religions out there. The Eastern religions tell us we'll lose ourselves in the Great Oneness. Islam says we'll live forever some place else, never to return to earth again. The atheist says once we're dead, that's it—just silence and dust.

Christainity says heaven is more like a layover than a destination. In the beginning of the Bible, in the book of Genesis, God creates the earth

---

[96] John 11:25.

as a home for us. At the end of the Bible, in the book of Revelation, God *remakes* the earth as a home for us.

We will be given new bodies. We will be resurrected the way Jesus was. And we will live on the earth forever. We will finally be Home.

It says at the end of Revelation (chapter 21) that the earth will be remade and that the City of God will come down out of heaven and be the New Jerusalem. The City of God will dwell among humans. Heaven and earth will be united because Jesus bridged the gap so we're no longer enemies of God. And we will live as God's friends on the earth with all the goodness we can enjoy forever.

OUR FIRST ENTRANCE

I once had a dream that I fell off a cliff. I hit the ground. I died. I could feel my soul slip away from my body, as if I was looking down on myself, and I puzzled over how weightless I felt.

I remember hearing that if you died in a dream, then you probably died in your sleep. How thankful I was the next morning when I discovered that this rumor wasn't true!

If my dream had kept going, what would have happened next? I often wonder. Yet regardless of the details, I cannot get out of my mind the fact that I will experience something that Tirian experienced after he walked through the stable door into the New Narnia.

The story is found in C.S. Lewis' *The Last Battle.* Eustace, Jill, Tirian, and many others had been fighting against the enemy who turned Narnia against itself. The Ape and Donkey impersonated the High King of Narnia, Aslan, by dressing up like a lion.

Tirian and the children were forced through the stable door, behind which a demonic monster would devour them.

But on the other side of the door, no monster greeted them. Instead they found themselves walking into a green meadow more pleasant than anything they'd ever seen in Narnia. Yet it also looked like Narnia.

As they moved about in this new world, every rock, tree, flower, and blade of grass looked as if it *meant* more.

They talked together, pointing out trees and animals, each thing more amazing than the last. Then a delicious scent filled the air. Another wonderful surprise.

Just then, Tirian turned to see where the scent was coming from. Before him, larger than life, stood all his heart's desire. Aslan himself drew near.

Tirian ruled the free peoples of Narnia, and he loved and served Aslan, even though he had never before met him face to face.

Until now.

This is one of the great meanings of "glory" in the Bible. It means to see something as it really is. And we share in glory when others see us as we really are, as whole, complete, healthy people.

John told us that this is what to expect when we see Jesus. "But we know that when Christ appears, we shall be like him, for we shall see him as he is."[97]

That, in essence, is what the Grand Entrance will be like. All the pleasures and goodness that we grew to love and appreciate in our lives on this earth will be there, each more amazing than the last as we finally understand their source. And then we will see him.

The One whom we have loved will come to us. There will be no need for words. All your heart's desires will be present in that moment. You'll stand eye to eye with the only One who really knows you, knows your story, knows your heartaches and your victories, knows the way others have misunderstood you, knows your pain and your tears, knows the diversions you've struggled with in your soul. He'll be there, inviting, welcoming, and warmly embracing. You'll be Home.

God will be our Home.

And then every day gets better than the one before. We'll learn and grow. Our souls' capacities to love will grow deeper and wider. We'll give love. We'll be more fully equipped to receive love. We'll better understand the mind of God. We'll better understand God's heart.

We'll worship him.

[97] 1 John 3:2.

WORSHIP

I used to ask, "How can I just go on worshiping God?" Wouldn't that get boring? I was imagining singing praise songs and hymns forever.

But here's the follow-up question, "What would God have to be like that you'd want to worship him forever?"[98]

He'd have to push the boundaries of my imagination!

I suggest that this is what God is like. And God will evoke worship from us that will flow from the depths of our souls. We'll find ourselves in the place where we finally feel like we belong—surrounded by love and understood. We'll want to worship, like a man wants to praise his woman, like a woman wants to love her man, like a mother wants to smile at her baby, and like a father wants to see his children succeed.

But that won't be all.

We'll worship God by enjoying his world. We'll worship God with our work. We'll worship God with our play. We'll worship God by loving one another. We'll worship God with our activities throughout every day and always. Worship will make sense of all of life. We'll welcome God's presence into everything because with him, everything will mean something more.

Heaven can begin now as we look to God instead of tinkering with our diversions. We can begin to walk with God, inviting him into our work and play. We can take pleasure in him in the very air we breathe.

We can find in God all our hearts' desires.

SAILING ON

As Gandalf tells Pippin during the great battle: "The journey doesn't end here. Death is just another path, one we all must take. The grey rain-curtain of this world rolls back, and all turns to silver glass. And then you see it."

"What, Gandalf? See what?" asked Pippin.

"White shores...and beyond, a far green country under a swift sunrise."

"Well, that isn't so bad," said Pippin.

"No...no it isn't," said Gandalf.[99]

We begin in the Wild and we live with our questions to help us get Home.

---

[98] Thanks to Dr. John Mark Reynolds for this question.

[99] From screenplay of *Lord of the Rings: The Return of the King*.

And once we're Home, we'll discover that the Wild was only the title page of our book. Chapter One will have just begun.[100]

QUESTIONS TO LIVE INTO

Which statement do you agree with? "I am a body; I have a soul" or "I am a soul; I have a body." Why?

Why is hell dead-bolted from the inside?

How does hell prove that God is fair?

What are you living more like today, heaven or hell? Why?

How do you need to re-understand eternal life as better quality? What would give your life better quality? How could God help you, specifically?

Read Isaiah 65 and Revelation 21. Compare the promises about a new heaven and earth. Which descriptions do you desire most? Why?

---

[100] Idea taken from C.S. Lewis and *The Last Battle*.

In this chapter, you read, "What would God have to be like that you'd want to worship him forever?" Answer that question for yourself. Do you believe God could be that great? Why or why not?

Are you a friend of God? Have you asked God to lead you out of the Wild? Have you trusted Jesus to wipe out your sins? If so, how has this chapter helped you understand death and heaven? If not, what's stopping you?

Notes

_____

_____

_____

_____

_____

_____

_____

_____

_____

_____

_____

_____

_____

The German poet, Ranier Maria Rilke, wrote to a younger poet a letter of encouragement, "Have patience with everything unresolved in your heart... Live the questions now. Perhaps then, someday far in the future, you will gradually, without even noticing it, live your way into the answer."[101]

A mentor of mine showed me that in college.

You and I have many more questions. And as we grow our questions will never become fully answered. As my friend, Dr. Jerry Root, says, "There are no final words. Only sure words. Everything can be plumbed a little deeper and understood a little wider." It's a journey of questions, after all.

And a journey of answers, too. When answers come, often a satisfaction comes as well that the puzzle pieces are falling into place. As we live with new questions, so we get to live with new answers.

When I was in graduate school, I was assigned to write a one-man show about a religious figure and perform it in front of 2,000 people. I chose Malcolm Muggeridge, the British journalist famous for uncovering Stalin's terror famine and for introducing the world to Mother Teresa.

In Muggeridge I found a deep questioner. And in him I found a context and a life through which to write my story.

Throughout his journey I threaded my own thoughts and struggles and reached a similar conclusion as Muggeridge. It's the Answer of answers to all my questions. This is what Muggeridge said when he found the Answer was a person:

> You not only give truth, you *are* truth. I see now why you give no answer. You yourself *are* the answer. I wrote and wrote page after page words that never became flesh. But you put meaning into this world with one indelible Word.[102]

That Word is Jesus Christ. There is enough evidence to know that he is here, and that he is giving Living Water to those who seek him. He's a King that men didn't crown and yet cannot dethrone. And he welcomes us to his Kingdom, one that men didn't build and yet cannot destroy.

He is a God who wears our wounds.

You are safe to live your questions with Jesus. And, as I have found, he gives freedom and strength to live the answers.

---

[101] Rainier Maria Rilke, *Letters to a Young Poet.*

[102] John 1:1, 14.

MORE QUESTIONS?

RESOURCES TO
INVESTIGATE

Note: The titles listed in bold are a bit easier to digest. All of the titles together represent starting points and will reference further sources to explore.

GENERAL

The Voyage of the Dawn Treader, C.S. Lewis

The Hobbit, J.R.R. Tolkien

The Lord of the Rings, J.R.R. Tolkien

Mere Christianity, C.S. Lewis

The Great Divorce, C.S. Lewis

Who Made God? And Answers to Over 100 Other Tough Questions of Faith, Ravi Zacharias and Norman L. Geisler (eds.)

EVIDENCE FOR THE BIBLE

Case for the Resurrection of Jesus, Gary R. Habermas and Michael R. Licona

The New Testament Documents: Are They Reliable? F.F. Bruce

Who Is This Jesus? Michael Green

SPIRITUAL GROWTH

Enjoy the Silence: A 30-Day Experiment in Listening to God, Duffy Robbins, Maggie Robbins

Wasting Time with God: A Christian Spirituality of Friendship with God, Klaus Issler and James Houston

When I Relax I Feel Guilty, Tim Hansel

CHRISTIAN DOCTRINES

Stand: Core Truths You Must Know for an Unshakable Faith, Alex McFarland

Heaven, Randy C. Alcorn

Velvet Elvis: Repainting the Christian Faith, Rob Bell

SEXUALITY AND DATING

Ruby Slippers, Jonalyn Fincher

Every Young Man's Battle, Stephen Arterburn and Fred Stoeker

Every Young Woman's Battle, Shannon Ethridge and Stephen Arterburn

Sex Is Not the Problem (Lust Is): Sexual Purity in a Lust-Saturated World, Joshua Harris

Questions You Can't Ask Your Mama about Sex, Craig Gross and Mike Foster

DIVORCE

Broken: Making Sense of Life after Your Parents Divorce, Tim Baker (*especially helpful is the chapter entitled "Lost Questions"*)

Generation Ex: Adult Children of Divorce and the Healing of Our Pain, Jen Abbas

CULTURE

Don't Buy the Lie: Discerning Truth in a World of Deception, Mark Matlock

Not the Way It's Supposed to Be: A Breviary of Sin, Cornelius Plantinga, Jr.

PHILOSOPHY

Smart Faith: Loving Your God with All Your Mind, J. P. Moreland and Mark Matlock (if you're ready for the next level, try *Love Your God with All Your Mind: The Role of Reason in the Life of the Soul,* J.P. Moreland)

WORLD RELIGIONS

The Illustrated Guide to World Religions, Dean C. Halverson

Why So Many Gods? Tim Baker

LIVING WITH QUESTIONS

ETHICS

Ethix: Being Bold in a Whatever World, Sean McDowell

Moral Choices, Scott B. Rae

SCIENCE

Moral Darwinism: How We Became Hedonists, Benjamin Wiker

The Language of God: A Scientist Presents Evidence for Belief,
Francis S. Collins